Blended
Beyond
Expectation

NAOMI L. HILL HUGH, MD

Author photo on back cover and page 244 by JCPenney Portraits.
Designed by Lisa Vega

The author would like to thank Bernai Brown Holman of Go Strong Fitness for permission to recount her guided imagery methodology in Chapter Eight, and to the Superior Court of New Jersey, Law Division, Family Part, Camden County for permission to reprint the court transcripts in Chapters Five and Seven. For further information contact the Hall of Justice, 101 South 5th Street, Camden, NJ 08103.

Printed in the United States of America

First edition 2020
Text has been registered with the Library of Congress. CIP data is on file.
ISBN: 978-1-7349310-0-6

To my adoring husband, Kelvin,
and three amazing sons,
Steffon, Justin, and Joshua

ACKNOWLEDGMENTS

With special thanks:

To Bishop David G. Evans for nurturing my spirit when it was dormant; for giving biblical counsel before marriage; for officiating my wedding ceremony; and for providing the sanctuary of Bethany Baptist Church in which my sons could flourish.

To Reverend Niki Brown, for not only seeing in me what others saw but for knowing how to draw it out, and see my more!

To Minister Cheryl N. Marion, for affording me the opportunity to free the little girl within and allow God's confident woman to soar.

To Pastor Joy Morgan, for creating the forum Write That Book!

To Hawa Jusu Johnson, for all God has created in you to inspire and encourage me to live empowered!

To Bernai Brown Holman, for allowing God to use your gift of imagery to birth my Nicodemus.

To my Women of Judah Dance Ministry sisters, for going beyond the veil on my behalf; for travailing with me in intercessory prayer and for creating a sisterhood that is more than just dance.

To my sister-friends, Lynda Singleton McClary, Dr. Gail A. McDonald, and Dr. Stephanie D. Sims Brown — for being there from the beginning of my becoming and for being a steady and strong yolk for my heavy burdens.

To my loving mother, Merdis E. Hill, for your steady guidance, unwavering support, and consistent confidence and for being the "grammar snob" who's influence is evident in everything I pen.

To Robert L. Hill, for being the man I'm proud to call my father. Your devotion, encouragement, and no-holds-barred conversations have helped me to resolve many difficult situations as a mother and wife.

To my elder brother, Darryl K. Hill, whose long-term circumstance taught me the meaning of true, sacrificial, sibling love.

To my younger brother, Brian P. Hill, for your super fluency with words, litigation skills, and gregarious personality that has strengthened our sibling tie and for the uncommon favor you've shown toward my firstborn, and how you add life to any family gathering.

To my entire extended family, for the DNA that connects us like no other relationship can.

To my Kressville Pediatrics family, for creating an environment that made working while wounded easy.

To Shana Murph, for allowing my voice to be heard through your gift of developmental editing.

To Jeannie Ng for your amazingly impeccable eye as a copy editor extraordinaire.

To Lisa Vega, for your gift of design that created this cover based on the title and our conversations before reading one word!

To my beloved husband, Kelvin H. Hugh, for being the lover of my soul, the one before whom I can confidently stand naked and unashamed, and for honoring our marriage covenant through the darkest of seasons.

To Steffon Aaron Crosswell Hugh, for relinquishing a huge portion of your father to me during a crucial point in your development and for creating a special place in your heart for "Mom2."

To Justin Elijah Hill, the firstborn from my womb, for teaching me to treasure my heart outside my body, for courageously walking the path God has planned for you and for allowing this audience to experience our transparency and vulnerability.

To Joshua Emmanuel Hugh, for being my patiently awaited, fervently prayed for, forty-year-old blessing of a son; the one who unites our blended family; the one who brightens our home and hearts each day; the one who completes my three sons; and for simply being my "Just Joshua."

And most importantly, to my God and Savior, Jesus Christ, for the opportunity to serve as Your ambassador on this Earth to fulfill Your intended will for my life and to present this work in obedience to Your instruction.

TABLE OF CONTENTS

I have been a mother for twenty-five years, a physician for twenty-four, and a wife for fourteen. The role for which I received the most complete, formidable, and predictable preparation was as a pediatrician.

I spent decades as a single Christian and married a Christian man. There was a specific, preconceived outcome we both anticipated to enjoy. We expected our sons to welcome, accept, and appreciate their new stepparent; we looked forward to birthing and raising our children in a home filled with the joy of the Lord; and we wanted our marriage to be a reflection of God's love and an example to other blended families. He expected genuine respect, and I, unconditional love.

Our union blended four hearts: ours and those of our two sons. What could have been more exciting?!

About fifteen years ago, I took a spiritual gifts test to see *where* I fit in the body of Christ. Several years later I took a personality assessment to see *how* my personality and spiritual gifts work together. Though I could not recall the specific results of either, I do remember thinking, "Oh, that makes perfect sense!"

It was not until retaking the test eighteen months ago that I saw *how* and *why* my life unfolded in the manner that it had. My top three spiritual gifts are giving, mercy, and discernment. It makes complete sense why the very nature of my being thrives on giving; my heart laments after mercy; and my spirit is inclined toward discernment.

Coping with the unexpected is difficult. Maneuvering through the potholes and valleys of a wounded heart is laborious. Allowing others into the crevices of your pain is challenging. I searched for books on blended families that addressed the challenges we faced. There were none. All I found were books on how to make the perfect blended family. My family was made. It was not perfect. In fact, it was being stretched far beyond any limits I could have imagined.

Many encouraged me to write this book. I began four years ago and then stopped. There was one word that stood between me and its completion: FEAR. I was afraid to reveal my heart and bare my soul. The irony was not that I had a fear of failure but of success.

Blended Beyond Expectation is a snapshot, a set

period, chosen and extracted from my life as a wife and mother. When I married, I did not expect the tug-of-war my heart would experience. Attempting to love and respect my husband while coping with intimate loss, and grasping to save a prodigal son, nearly crushed my spirit. I was exhausted and desperate, but no one could tell. I functioned behind a mask of confident strength, holding my marriage and family together by the threads of faith and hope, believing in total restoration.

I invite you on a journey through your own heart. I encourage you to pause and reflect, to release and embrace, to let go and accept. You will be given pearls of wisdom to transition from a place of insecurity, lack and defeat, into a place of confidence, abundance, and victory.

It is my prayer that you experience the sincere devotion and faithful encouragement of a husband after his wife suffers a devastating loss; that you mourn with a mother who finds the courage to pray for her son to hit rock-bottom; and that you see the redeeming love of a faithful Father, which restored the heart of that beloved son.

This book is best read in sequence with a pen, paper, and tissue in hand. Each chapter is followed by a Devotional Anecdote, Questions to Consider, Words of

Encouragement, a Song for Your Season, and an Act of Kindness.

The devotionals highlight a woman in the Bible whose life corresponds best with the season in which I found myself. I compare her life to my circumstance to teach a lesson. These lessons are intended to develop inner strength and confidence.

In Questions to Consider, there are four questions designed to make you think deeply to cause you to look insightfully at a season that has already passed or one in which you currently find yourself. They lend themselves nicely for journaling. Take time after each chapter to dwell in the moment. Have a conversation with yourself. Allow yourself space to begin the healing process before moving on.

Everyone needs words of encouragement. Whatever your "it" is, you are not in it alone. I believe these words will fall gently in your place of barrenness, be watered by the tears of your pain, and produce the fruit of increase and restoration in your due season.

Often the melody of a song lifts our spirits, and the lyrics are meat to our souls. Our minds dance with pleasure and our bodies jump for joy. Ah, to be lost in the moment! Music can transcend time. I have included a song that spoke directly to my heart and nourished my soul in the center of my season. Seize the opportunity for music to heal your brokenness.

How many times do you carry out good deeds for others but neglect yourself? It's easier to see a need in someone else than the person looking back at you in the mirror. I challenge every reader to perform an act of kindness toward themselves or another. I implore you to practice self-centeredness! When flying on an airplane, should the cabin pressure drop, you are instructed to secure your own oxygen mask before assisting others. We know this, but it is not always our first response. After reading each chapter, make this your first response.

Marianne Williamson wrote this regarding fear: "Our deepest fear is not that we are inadequate. Our deepest fear is that we are powerful beyond measure. It is our light, not our darkness that most frightens us."

Don't be afraid to take this journey with me. I challenge you to overcome your fear and: Face. Everything. And. Rise!

CHAPTER ONE

†

Who's Running This House?

S ince second grade, I only ever wanted to become a
pediatrician. I accepted Christ at eight years old,
and He's charted my life's course to that end. At
age twenty-five, I entered Howard University College of
Medicine and was on my way to actualizing this dream.
During that time, I met a man with whom I conceived a
son. In October 1994, Justin was born near the beginning
of my third year. With an eye toward proficiency and a
compulsion for order, my dean and I devised a plan for
me to remain enrolled and graduate with my class. And
that I did, with my nineteen-month-old son by my side.

Though a physician and mother, I knew well that I
had done things out of order as a Christian. The thought
of being counted among the statistics of single women
giving birth in Washington, D.C., in 1994 made me
angry. The relationship between Justin's father and I
ended before Justin was born. Because I had sinned
sexually before God, I felt shamed. I disappointed my

maturing cousins, who all looked up to me as a godly example. I apologized and made a vow before God and them: I would never defile my body, my temple of the Holy Spirit, ever again before marriage. I would never do what it took to create life again until my wedding night.

After graduating from medical school, I moved back to New Jersey, where I was a postgraduate resident in the Department of Pediatrics at Cooper Hospital, and very close to family. Though elated to be back home, and exceptionally busy with work and single parenting, I felt a void in my personal life. I didn't always want to be single, nor did I want a man to feel I was looking for a father for my son. He had a father. We were just not a family. I entered a respectful, loving relationship with a Christian man, William, whom I'd known since high school. Our immediate and extended families were members of the same church, Parkside United Methodist in Camden. Nevertheless, over many years, we tried off and on, we concluded the relationship was one of safety and would never grow into marriage. It seemed to flourish by being platonic rather than romantic. After three years, I graduated from my residency program and joined Kressville Pediatrics. It was a private pediatric practice run by a solo practitioner with two office locations.

Justin was getting older, and our current church was no longer satisfying my spiritual needs. Despite my being a co-youth adviser, there remained a void in meeting the specific spiritual needs of the youth. Nonetheless, it was where my family worshipped, so I was hesitant to leave. On Sunday, June 10, 2001, I was invited to Bethany Baptist Church, in Lindenwold, New Jersey, to attend the baby dedication of one of my high school classmates. I was fully engaged the entire time. From the hospitality to the praise and worship, to the depth of the preached Word, to the presence of the Holy Spirit, I was captivated, and so was Justin! I knew from the very first time I entered the sanctuary, my destiny was connected to this church. For the next two months, we attended Bethany at eight a.m. and Parkside at eleven a.m. In submission to the Holy Spirit's yielding, on the second Sunday in August, I joined Bethany. We attended Parkside at eleven a.m., and as is our family's custom, we gathered at Mum-Mum's following service. I remember the conversation as though it were yesterday.

"MumMum, I joined Bethany today."

"Well, Naomi. How are you going to be a member of two churches at the same time?"

"MumMum, I'm not."

"But what about the youth?"

"Roxanne is there. She can handle the youth. I don't know how to explain it. But my destiny is at that church!"

I made a promise to myself and Justin that I would not bring another man into my life unless he intended to marry me and parent him. For the next five years, I worked to provide every need we would encounter and fulfill the many desires our hearts could imagine. When he turned seven, we celebrated his birthday in a newly constructed townhome. My drive, constancy, and stick-to-it-iveness paid off. I was an "Amazon Woman." A warrior woman who had accomplished it all. I had a fantastic job, a peaceful home, belonged to a thriving church, and had truly found contentment in my singleness.

I decided to hold God to the promises in my life's Scripture: Delight yourself also in the Lord, and He shall give you the desires of your heart. Commit your way to the Lord; trust also in Him; and He shall bring it to pass (Psalms 37:4-5). I delighted and trusted in Him daily and was living a repented and committed life. The next step was to talk to Him about my heart's desire, and that I did. I began reading *The Power of a Praying Wife* by Stormie Omartian and visualized my future husband: a tall thin man of medium complexion with mixed gray hair; eyes that would be inviting; and a smile that brightened my day. Pleasing the Lord would be more important than pleasing me; in fact, he'd be willing to do backflips for his Lord. His dress would be one of class and distinction, down to his socks and shoes; respect and love for his mother would be evident without a spoken word; he would be gainfully employed and fiscally responsible; he would be well-spoken and his character would be without flaw; he may or may not have children—if so, he would love them unconditionally and provide for them sufficiently; and his commitment to marriage, covering my son, and enjoying the fruit of my womb would be our great joy. With that, I prayed, and sat still at His feet with my heart and mind focused on His will.

Kelvin grew up during the 1960s in Trenton, New Jersey. Upon high school graduation, he earned a certificate as an electronics technician in radio and television repair. He worked to pay his way through community college and graduated with an associate's degree in humanities and social sciences.

During the '70s, he was a member of the East Trenton Civic Association and fought strongly and proudly as a community activist. The election of school board members and city councilmen was as crucial as confronting dilapidated housing and pursuing missing property owners. One of his most honored assignments was canvassing for Kenny Gibson. Kenneth A. Gibson was the first African American elected mayor of any northeastern United States city: Newark, New Jersey. A member of the Democratic Party, he ran as New Jersey's first Black governor. Unfortunately, he did not achieve the majority vote.

Looking for stability and job security, Kelvin, at age twenty-nine, joined the New Jersey State Department of Corrections as an officer. His commitment toward provision and stewardship led him to purchase a single-family home several years later. His home was a welcoming gathering place for holidays and family celebrations. And he had a big family: an identical twin brother; six sisters; and a host of nieces, nephews, and cousins. In November 1993, at the age of thirty-seven, he became a single father to his son, Steffon. Realizing his desire to marry and bring a wife into his home, he maintained his house well and did not allow others to defile it.

He too was in a relationship that dissolved while his son was very young. Sometime in 1994, a woman he was dating invited him to attend Bethany Baptist Church. He was not a Christian. He attended simply to be with her. After a while, he began to read the Bible and understand

God for himself. By the summoning of the Holy Spirit, a desire to live a changed life, and revelation of the preached Word, in 1996, he accepted Bishop David G. Evan's invitation and joined the church. The following year, he accepted Christ as his personal Lord and Savior. As a result, he was convicted in his current dating relationship. It was not one that honored the Lord since he found himself engaging in sexual sin. Though both were now Christians, he fulfilled the role of leader and decided to cease the acts of fornication. He was so committed to living a lifestyle of holiness that he went to the altar and asked God to take away his sexual desire until marriage. The young woman he was dating did not agree with waiting until marriage. The relationship dissolved.

As a single Christian man, he served in ministry. He joined the Kingdom Guards, Haven Singles Ministry, and the Children's Ministry. His desire to live a changed life kept him focused on the things of God and not the distractions of the world. For the next five years, he maintained his focus and cultivated a relationship with his son and his heavenly Father.

January 2002 was the beginning of a new year. Though a member at Bethany for five months, I was comfortable, but not settled. I became involved with the

Single Parent and Singles Ministries while Justin was active in the Children's and SAGE Mentoring Ministries. To meet new people, I attended a winter ball sponsored by the Singles Ministry. One of the icebreakers was introducing yourself to three people you did not know and telling three things about yourself. One of the people I met was Kelvin Hugh. His stature and smile caught me off-guard; I blushed. Another was Carla McGruder. I do not recall the third. We three, along with, five others sat together at a table for eight. Because Carla was a dentist and lived in the same development and on the same street as me, we wound up talking most of the evening, and I would glance in Kelvin's direction periodically. The night was filled with food, fellowship, entertainment, and dancing. I enjoyed the ball and was glad I had attended. I was disappointed because I opted to get to know Carla rather than Kelvin, better. After all, Bethany has thousands of members and two services each Sunday. When would our paths ever cross again?

After a few weeks, we met again as he volunteered in the Children's Church. From time to time, we'd see each other when I signed Justin in or out. I secretly looked forward to those happenstances.

The Travel Ministry announced a seven-day cruise

to the southern Caribbean in August 2003. Perfect. I needed a vacation and would love to go. I'd feel safe traveling with a group from the church. If I wanted to be around people, great. If I wanted time alone, great. I would be accountable and accounted for. Sign me up!

As the months passed, my faith, commitment, and understanding of God grew. Each Sunday morning sermon, I felt God spoke directly to me. Questions I pondered were answered. The decisions I needed to make were made clear. I was a better mother. Spiritually and relationally, I was a stronger woman. My purpose and destiny were tied to that church. I was settled comfortably, awaiting their reveal.

Two weeks before departure, there was a mandatory meet and greet for those going on the cruise. Fantastic. I would finally get to meet my cabinmate. I opted for a double rather than a single cabin. Our names had been exchanged before the trip, but because she lived in Delaware, we had not yet met. An even greater surprise was that Kelvin was going on the cruise, and yes, he was at the meet and greet. I said, "I didn't know you were going on this cruise." His reply: "I didn't know you were going either." We traded expressions of unexpected approval woven, with pleasurable intrigue. Bon voyage!

We cruised from San Juan to Saint Thomas, Saint Maarten, Antigua, Saint Lucia, and Barbados, and enjoyed one day at sea. The island views were breathtaking from every vantage point; and the food, delicious. When we disembarked in Saint Lucia, some of us were surprised to see that a group of us had signed up for the same excursion. The attraction Kelvin and I felt as we endured a meandering ride to the top of a volcano was epitomized as we beheld the spectacular views overlooking the majestic blue sea. It was as if we were the only ones on the excursion. We enjoyed lunch before visiting a black-sand beach and, finally, snorkeling. We were the only two in our group who decided to snorkel. The butterflies I felt thus far were instantly replaced by the feeling of a bottomless pit. You see, to snorkel, you had to provide identifying information before obtaining your gear. Kelvin completed the information first. When it was my turn, I could see what he wrote: name, Birth Date, Ship, and Cabin Number. That's it. Game over. I'm doomed. Well, the feelings were nice while they lasted. I quickly did the math in my head. He was eleven years my senior. He was going to think I was a baby. I was disappointed, and we geared up and went out while the rest of our group enjoyed the beach.

Later, after returning to the ship, Kelvin invited me to dinner. We decided on Johnny Rockets. Our conversation was more intentional and personal than it had been before. I confessed I had looked at his birth date and determined our age difference. He assured me it was not a problem for him. Further dialogue revealed he was a corrections officer. I told him I was a pediatrician. He felt disqualified when I told him my profession. I assured him it was not a problem for me. We were pleasantly surprised to know we were the single parents of sons who were eleven months apart. I nearly fell off the chair when he replied, "Across the hall," when I asked, "How far do you live from your mother?" Good Lord. Not another grown man living at home with his momma. This was surely a disqualifier for me. Amused by the look on my face (which I thought I had cleverly hid), he clarified, "She lives with me." The meal and remainder of the conversation were enjoyable. Exhausted from the day, but wanting to continue getting to know each other, we decided to rest and refresh, and meet again for dancing at ten p.m.

Eleven thirty p.m.! Oh no, I overslept. I quickly made my way to the disco, where a group of us had gathered to dance the night away. Refreshed, Kelvin and I were a suitable match on the dance floor, and danced until closing. Not ready to call it a night, we walked around the upper deck. We came upon an outdoor soccer game and settled against a railing overlooking a court. Before we knew it, we'd talked for two hours. It was there, as Thursday, August 7, turned into Friday, August 8, cruising on the Caribbean Sea, somewhere between Saint Lucia and Barbados, that the supernatural happened. Like Elizabeth with child in the presence of Mary carrying Jesus, something within my spirt leapt in the presence of his. I didn't understand it, but I certainly appreciated it. I was smitten by the sparkle in his eye and the gleam of his smile. He walked me to my cabin and then we bid each other a good night. I shall never forget Saint Lucia.

Over the next few months, I found myself thinking of Kelvin often. As amicable thoughts toward him increased, so did those of insecurity and doubt. I vacillated between allowing myself to feel positively about the possibility of a new relationship, and returning to the safe and familiar one. It was an uncomfortable place to abide. Desiring emotional peace, on October 30, I met with William. During lunch at Ruby Tuesday, I told him of my Caribbean experience, and I finally put an end to the on and off relationship I had with him. In disbelief of the inevitable, he reluctantly accepted. However, on

November 24, first thing in the morning, we engaged in an uncomfortably heated and emotionally draining telephone conversation. I was left in a place of bewilderment and abandonment, feeling emotionally wounded and mentally exhausted. We ended the discussion with apologies and a notion to agree to disagree.

As I read my morning devotion, Day 24, "Transformed by Truth" from *The Purpose Driven Life*, I found myself in a pool of tears, confusion, mental pain, spiritual wilderness, and emotional turmoil. My entire countenance was troubled. I could not stop crying. The breakup had been so difficult. My mind was racing from one thought to the next. I desperately needed a hug—for someone to physically wrap their arms around my body. Nothing and no one was here for me. At this moment, I could not even feel the comfort of the Holy Spirit.

Soon it was time to leave for work. I was so distraught and bewildered that driving was a difficult task. It was just the Lord and me. I cried out to Him for help. I pushed in a Donnie McClurkin CD and began to listen. And at eight forty-five a.m., the words to "Create in Me a Clean Heart" began to minister to me: "Create in me a clean heart and purify me . . . so I may worship You." After that, I asked the Holy Spirit to come into my vehicle and comfort me. I cried out in such a way that my body shook in pain. The emotional turmoil was deep down in the core of my being. I needed a hug from my Father God. I was left with no one to turn to but Him. The very moment I asked for comfort, I felt it. The dense gray cloud over me was lifted to reveal a fluffy white one. The air was clear and blue. I felt a fresh anointing covering me. I pulled into the parking lot. Six and a half miles and seventeen minutes later, I'd made it.

When lunchtime came, I was still troubled in my spirit. I decided to leave the building in search of a quite place to park. As I drove, I received a call from him again. He was calling to see how I was holding up. It was more than I could bear at that moment. I reached the football field where my son played. I pulled up to the gate, just beyond the nearest goalpost, and parked. Although he tried to talk me through this bewilderment. I ended the call. At that very moment, amid all my tears and sobs, I heard the Lord speak. He very plainly said, "Stop talking. Just listen." He said it about three times. I finally said, "I can't talk. I have to go. I cannot talk." In the silence, with the bright sun beaming through the windshield, I wailed unto the Lord. I totally surrendered to Him and waited for Him to speak again. I confessed I could do nothing without Him. I needed Him now more than ever. I needed direction, wisdom, and guidance. As I looked at the clock—it was one fifteen p.m.—the Lord again said, "Be quiet and listen." Then the sobbing stopped. He continued, "Listen." So, I pushed the power button on the CD player to listen to Donnie McClurkin again. Now, these are the words that brought me comfort:

> *"Again I call you and again you answer*
> *Again I need you and again you're there*
> *Again I reach out and again you hold me*
> *You console me once more, and again."*

This is the very first song on the CD as well, the title track "Again." The Lord led me by His Spirit to the last song on the CD. I recorded the lyrics in a journal. At one thirty p.m., I was ministered to by these words:

> *"He's calling you.*
> *Tell me what are you going to do?*
> *Your time has come for life brand new.*
> *He's calling you."*

He spoke to me one more time,

> *"Prepare yourself to be his wife."*

What? Did I hear Him correctly? 'Prepare yourself to be his wife?' I had the most ambivalent feeling you could imagine: the abiding peace and comfort of His

Spirit and the weighted fear and disbelief of my mind.

The next thing I knew, it was time to return to work. As I drove along the five-mile distance, I replayed this song over and over. I said yes to Jesus and His call on my life. Yes to all He had spoken to me in my wilderness. For the first time, He had completely isolated and stilled me, even from my tears, to speak a word into and over my life. This entire experience was a confirmation of what had been revealed to me since April. All that relates to personal growth, spiritual maturity, destiny, vision, and purpose had just been confirmed. And, as if that was not enough, the next morning's devotion, Day 25, *The Purpose Driven Life,* was titled "Transformed by Trouble."

As I began to share my experience with select people, I knew the Lord was placing me in a position to be blessed. I began to fast and pray very specifically for the Lord to prepare me for the next dimension in my life and in Him. I also asked Him to prepare those who would accompany me along this journey. By no means had I shared the final words the Lord had spoken to me with Kelvin. However, I was obedient in preparation. I read many books, including some of my favorites titles: the Understanding Love series and *Single, Married, Separated, and Life After the Divorce,* by Dr. Myles Monroe;

His Needs, Her Needs, by Willard F. Harley Jr.; *What Every Man Wants in a Woman*; *What Every Woman Wants in a Man,* by John and Diana Hagee; *What to Do Until Love Finds You* and *In Search of the Proverb 31 Man,* by Michelle McKinney Hammond; *What to Do Before You Say "I Do,"* by Stenneth Powell; and probably every woman's favorite *Knight in Shining Armor,* by P. B. Wilson.

For an entire year, Kelvin and I exchanged Sunday morning pleasantries before eventually exchanging phone numbers and then formally dating. On our first date, we took our sons to the Winter Lights, a Christmas Light show at Six Flags Great Adventure. We moved slowly through our courtship. So much so that it took him a full eleven months to kiss me. Yes, eleven months! I had begun to feel he wasn't as interested in me as I was in him. It was the July fourth weekend and he came over for a visit. He kissed me good-bye on the way out the door. Oh, did the fireworks explode! I became so overwhelmed with emotion, I waited for him to drive off before I ran into the house, closed the door, and began screaming, crying, and jumping up and down. He liked me! He liked me! He really did like me! I began praying and walking through my house, rebuking the presence and power of the Enemy. I knew, from that very moment, He would come against our relationship. Kelvin had a thirty-minute drive and always called after arriving home safely, and this night was no different. Bashfully I asked, "Why did it take you so long to kiss me?" He replied, "Because I know me. It does not have anything to do with you. I know how far I can go before I cannot handle myself. I respect you too much to put you in a compromising position. I had to wait until I got to a point where I was strong enough to manage the feelings that are going to get stirred up." My heart simply melted.

We dated for two years, and there were several crucial things to which I had paid close attention: His relationship with the Lord, his son, my son, and his mother. All were consistent, purposeful, and sincere. My son got along well with his, and vice versa. My parents and brother approved of him as a suitable and deserving mate for me. During our courtship, he was ordained deacon. With permission from my father, on August 23, 2005, he proposed over dinner at the ChopHouse in Gibbsboro, New Jersey. And I said yes! We picked a wedding date and scheduled premarital counseling with our pastor. We were pleased to know those sessions would include us, with and without our sons, and our sons, without us. We were excited and prepared for this engagement season.

On Saturday, June 3, 2006, with my father at my side, I stood at the back of the sanctuary in a white, sequined-and-beaded halter gown, with a two-tier veil—the second layer was draped from a tiara and was brought forward to cover my face, and the first layer was cathedral length and flowed over the train of my dress. Candelabras with tall white candles showed their flickering flames as they lined the center aisle and altar. I looked beyond our guests to behold Kelvin, smiling and standing tall in a white tuxedo jacket, vest, shirt, and tie; black pants and shoes, with a white calla lily and baby's breath pinned to his left lapel. The groomsmen and bridesmaids, in their sapphire and light blue, stood in anticipation. With Bishop Evans's acknowledgment and the playing of Allen and Allen's "I Prayed for You", the guests rose, and I walked humbly and intentionally, escorted by my father, down the center aisle. There was no semblance of anxiety, doubt, or regret. I had prepared and was ready to become Mrs. Kelvin Hill Hugh.

Our guests cheered as we entered the reception dancing confidently to "Ain't No Stoppin' Us Now", by McFadden and Whitehead. From our first dance, "Answer to My Prayer", by Allen and Allen, to the last—and each one in between—we celebrated what God orchestrated.

Our wedding night was a beautifully expressed culmination of two lives lived sacrificially, and committed to the Lord. I was his spotless bride, and he, my spotless groom. Our hearts danced and sang as we consummated our marriage and beheld each other as the man and woman in the Song of Solomon. We honeymooned in Maui and returned to New Jersey to live happily ever after.

Although we had purchased homes of our own, we knew we would ultimately live in one and sell the other. The obvious solution was for me to move into his and sell mine. For me, this option brought to light several concerns. First, his home was too far away from the hospitals and offices where I worked. My twenty-minute commute would more than double. Second, I was Justin's custodial parent. This move would cause him to be displaced from his school district and community of friends. Even more, it would cost him *his* home. And, lastly, Kelvin's house was older, less spacious, and much farther from our church.

Conversely, him moving into my home revealed several concerns for him. One, he was to be the head of the home. He felt this was an additional challenge to moving into my home. Two, he was the man. The provider. He had purchased and maintained a home with the express purpose of providing for his future wife and children. Third, Justin, although only eleven, had served as the alpha male in his own home. Kelvin moving into my home was nearly certain to produce territorial friction.

My immediate thoughts were of my struggle and sacrifice to provide a very nice home for myself and Justin. I did not want to do what I felt was a downgrade. Kelvin planned to retire within five years. He could withstand the longer commute and reside in my home. My "Amazon Woman" instincts were in full warrior mode. This was not a transition I was willing to assume. I felt my happiness and Justin's well-being were of greater importance.

Kelvin is a man, period. He did not desire to move into a woman's home. As a church leader, the Bible says, he must manage his family well. If he did not know how to manage his own family, how could he take care of God's church (1 Timothy 3:4-5)? His main concern was providing for his family and ruling his home properly.

After much focused prayer, we decided he would move into my home and prepare his for sale. Some of the profits from that sale would be put toward the principal of my home. After an additional year, we would sell my home and move into a home that was ours. There would no longer be "his, mine, and ours". Just "ours". As fate would have it, the housing market crashed in 2007. His house was on the market for an entire year. The price had been lowered a few times, and we decided he was not *giving* it away. We took it off the market and became landlords. At this point, since we had been living in my home, once the market recovered, either home would be considered for first sale.

God honored our sacrifice of abstinence until marriage, for me, since March 1994, and Kelvin since 2001. Our reward was the announcement of my pregnancy, after marriage, on Christmas morning 2006. Kelvin's eyes were wide and glistening as he said, "My wife is pregnant!" August 2007 brought the addition of baby Joshua. He was a prayed for and much anticipated welcome to our family. By now, Justin and Steffon were nearly thirteen and fourteen years old, respectively. We were more than happy to boast of our three sons.

We were living happily ever after until the struggle for male dominance became evident. Steffon, whose mother was the primary custodian, rebelled against his father's marriage by not visiting as often as he used to. There were times Kelvin went to pick him up, and Steffon would refuse to come out of the house. Or he would get into the car, only to exit once his father entered the driver's seat. Steffon wished his father had remained single until he graduated high school. Although I was loving and attentive, he did not need, nor was he interested in, a stepmother. It put an unfamiliar strain on a previously vibrant and healthy relationship between a father and his son. This loving father had become temporarily separated from his biological son's bond, only to live in daily competition with the preadolescent, ego-tripping son of the woman he loves.

Justin had begun to reject Kelvin's presence since he felt he did not need nor want a stepfather in the home. What began as subtle innuendos regarding simple salutations had escalated from there. Justin would say to Kelvin, "Why do you have to ask how my day was at school?" "Why do you have to ask me if I have homework? My mom will ask me when she gets home." "I don't need to ask your permission to do this. I already know my mom would say yes." "Man, you don't have to tell me to clean my room or do my chores. My mom tells me to do that." As the tension between them mounted, the verbiage became more hostile. "You can just leave here. We can be nice to each other, but you don't have to act like my dad. I already have a dad." Or I would be asked, "Why can't you have your own opinion anymore? If I ask you where we're going to eat dinner, and you pick a restaurant, why do you change your mind when Kelvin suggests something different? Like, you used to think for yourself. Now, you act like you're afraid to say something different than him. What happened to you since you got married?" As fear of losing control loomed, he grew more desperate. "This is our house. He's not in charge here. You are! Why did you move him in here anyway? He has his own house. He could just live there and visit here on weekends or something. He can just go, but he's leaving my little brother here." It was as if we were in a tornado, and it appeared the roof was about to be blown right off the house.

Kelvin felt disrespected. I was ashamed. Justin sensed betrayal. Kelvin wanted me to control my son. I expected Justin to obey my husband. Justin longed to have me all to himself. Kelvin was ready to leave, and Justin wanted him to go. I was caught in the middle like a frayed rope.

Who's running this house?!

DEVOTIONAL ANECDOTE:

A LESSON FROM RUTH

†

The story of Ruth is one of love, devotion, and redemption.

Ruth was from Moab. The Moabites are the descendants of Lot, founded from an incestuous relationship between Lot and his oldest daughter. She got him drunk and slept with him to produce an heir. The Kingdom was full of those who practiced sexual sins, witchcraft, and warfare. They were disobedient worshippers of pagan gods, faithless, and they were not allowed to enter the congregation of the Lord, even to their tenth generation.

Ruth was the daughter-in-law of Naomi and sister-in-law of Orpah. All three were widows. Naomi's husband died first. After ten years of marriage, her sons, Mahlon and Chilion, died. Without a husband or sons, Naomi became bitter. She had left Bethlehem full and was ready to return empty. Orpah remained in Moab, hoping to find another husband and have children. Ruth, though poor and desolate with neither husband nor son to give her social status or value, chose to stay with Naomi. She told Ruth, "Wherever you go, I will go; wherever you lodge, I will lodge. Your people shall be my people, and your God shall be my God. Where you die, I will die, and there will I be buried. Only death will separate us." She was willing to give up her people and her culture to follow Naomi.

They journeyed and reached Bethlehem during the barley harvest. Naomi had a kinsman of her husband's family, named Boaz. He was a mighty man of wealth, approximately twenty years Ruth's senior, whose name meant, "in Him is strength." Ruth asked Naomi permission to gather ears of corn on the threshing floor in his field that she might find favor in his sight. This turned out to be humiliating, as she could gather only the shears left over after the reapers had filled their baskets.

Boaz noticed her and asked who she was. He was told she was a Moabite damsel who returned with Naomi. Nevertheless, he told Ruth to gather only in his fields, stay close to his maidens, and drink from the vessels that the young men had drawn. And he charged the young men not to touch her. He allowed her to eat and drink, seated beside the reapers, until she was full. Not only was she permitted to gather after the reapers, but that some handfuls of corn should fall on purpose, and she was not to be blamed or rebuked.

Boaz became Ruth's kinsman-redeemer. He was related to her as if by blood. He was able to pay the price for her redemption, and he was willing to redeem her. He himself was free. He married Ruth, and they bore a son, Obed. Boaz transformed her from widowhood and poverty to marriage and wealth. He brought a Moabite woman into David's bloodline, and eventually to Christ, as Obed was the grandfather of David.

Though Ruth gathered the leftovers, she still reaped a harvest. She was a virtuous woman of integrity and righteousness, who lived above the standard of her day. She is an example of God's faithfulness amid a faithless nation. Scripture does not offer us a sanctified view of life. God works with broken and sinful people right where they are. He does not try to mask problems or hide flaws. Even Jesus was born into a dysfunctional family!

Like Ruth, I chose to leave Moab, where sexual sin, disobedience, and moral decay ran rampant. I had to renegotiate friendships, change social venues, and commit to walking the walk and not simply talking the talk.

Because of my humility and devotion, God favored me with His kinsman-redeemer, Kelvin Hugh. Like Boaz, Kelvin was able, willing, and free to pay the price for my redemption. He was not worried about protecting me from younger men, he was worried about protecting me from himself. I sat beside him at the table while he led a life exemplifying respect, virtue, love, and godliness until I was fully satisfied. Our relationship was sanctified before God, despite a past riddled with brokenness and flaws.

Kelvin married me, and we became a blended family. God blessed our union with a son, Joshua. Now, we are on a path purposed to live out His plan for our lives. It did not yet appear who Joshua would be—as it seems he was born into a dysfunctional family!

QUESTIONS TO CONSIDER

1. What life event has left you widowed?
2. What decisions have you made that would alter your destiny forever?
3. Are you quiet enough to hear God when He speaks?
4. Can God trust you to follow Him?

WORDS OF ENCOURAGEMENT

"Delight yourself also in the Lord, and He shall give you the desires of your heart. Commit your way to the Lord, trust also in Him, and He shall bring it to pass." (Psalm 37:4-5).

SONG FOR YOUR SEASON

"He's Calling You" —Donnie McClurkin

ACT OF KINDNESS

No matter your age or station in life, find yourself a spiritual mentor.

CHAPTER TWO

†

Inauguration Day

Illinois state senator Barack Obama blazed onto the political scene at the 2004 Democratic National Convention when he presented the keynote address. About four months after the October 2006 release of his book *The Audacity of Hope*, on February 10, 2007, Obama announced his presidential campaign run with a slogan he first used in his 2004 senatorial campaign: "Yes We Can." On Tuesday, November 4, 2008, the Democratic Party–nominee Senator Barack Obama and running mate Senator Joe Biden defeated Republican Party–nominee Senator John McCain and running mate Governor Sarah Palin to become the forty-fourth president and forty-seventh vice president, respectively, of the United States of America.

Tuesday, January 20, 2009, was the first inauguration of Barack H. Obama II. There was excitement in the air. We gathered Justin and Joshua and cozied up on the sofa in front of the television to witness history unfold:

the swearing-in ceremony of the first African American president. It was a chilling twenty-eight degrees in Washington, D.C. Dr. Rick Warren delivered the invocation; Aretha Franklin sang "My Country, 'Tis of Thee"; a performance of John Williams's composition "Air and Simple Gifts", was rendered by the quartet made up of: cellist Yo-Yo Ma, violinist Itzhak Perlman, pianist Gabriela Montero, and clarinetist Anthony McGill. At 12:05 p.m., with his left hand atop Abraham Lincoln's Bible, and his right raised, Barack H. Obama repeated the Presidential Oath of Office administered by Chief Justice John G. Roberts Jr. Surrounded by the First Family— wife Michelle, and daughters Malia and Natasha "Sasha" —President Obama addressed a global audience with the inaugural theme "a new era of responsibility."

We absorbed the emotions of the day. Following the luncheon and parade were the many balls of the evening. During such celebratory pomp and circumstance, I snuck upstairs to take a home pregnancy test. How wonderful would it be to announce the addition of a new member to the Hugh family? It was four weeks since my last cycle, and we had been trying to conceive. As I waited in anticipation, the testing stick revealed two blue lines: Pregnant! What?! Could it be that I would forever be able to say, "I found out I was pregnant the same day the first African American president was sworn into office?" Was I really going to have another baby? Would this be the girl I've wanted for so long? Was Joshua going to be a big brother? This was thrilling! With excitement, I sashayed down the steps into the family room to share this wonderful news. "Joshua is going to be a big brother."

Kelvin asked, excitedly, "Are you pregnant?!"

"Yes, yes, I am pregnant!" We hugged, kissed, and embraced our sons as we reveled in the celebration of the day.

"Next month I will be forty-two years old. If You were faithful to bless Sarah's womb in her old age, surely You can bless mine. I trust and believe Your Word, 'Delight thyself also in the Lord, and He shall give thee the desires of thine heart.' Please God, bless the fruit of my womb. This is Your child and I am honored You have once again chosen me as the vessel through which to bring this child into this world. Thank You for blessing our marriage and our obedience to Your Word. I commit their life to You, even as they grow and develop within. Help me be a good steward over my body until I birth them into this world. Thank You for allowing us to have our very own Inauguration Day. In Your name I pray, Amen."

My birthday always coincides with Valentine's Day

weekend. That year, we celebrated by attending a marriage conference called "Weekend to Remember®," presented by FamilyLife in Hershey, Pennsylvania. It was the perfect opportunity to build upon and strengthen our marriage's biblical foundation, while enjoying much needed "we" time. On my birthday, February 13, we arrived in Hershey and were amazed to witness eight hundred couples in attendance. That Friday evening's topics included "Why Marriages Fail" and "Can We Talk?" We learned levels of communication are directly proportional to degrees of transparency, and how well we listen allows us to focus on what is being said, not on the way it is being said. You should never think with your emotions because they cannot think. Our homework for the night was to share our feelings and commitment with each other through an interactive exercise.

Saturday's sessions were "Unlocking the Mysteries of Marriage," "We Fight Too," and "Marriage After Dark." We learned that marriage should mirror God's image, mutually complete one another, and multiply a godly legacy. We leave to cleave and become one flesh; not giving fifty-fifty of ourselves, but rather 100 percent. Blending differences and weaknesses into one flesh requires challenging Satan's opposing forces as his focus is on independence separate from God. Our homework assignment was three-fold: spend time in prayer, write a love letter (writing the answers to specific questions), and go on a date.

A love letter to my husband, Kelvin

2-14-09

When we first met, I was attracted to your beautiful bright smile, sparkling mixed grey hair, and well put together physical appearance. I watched you as you interacted with people around you and later with your son. I was deeply moved by the way you parented him as a single father. You constantly sacrificed your time and money crossing the bridge into Philadelphia, traveling back to New Jersey, just to have Steffon in your home; and back and forth across the bridge again, before coming home to rest. What a commitment. Not to mention, the evenings you had to go to church for Bible study, a meeting, or to serve as a Kingdom Guard.

Since we've been married, I've seen you become frustrated with the effects of a blended family. Even though there have been times I had to painfully endure hearing, "This is not what I signed up for. If things don't change, I'm out of here." Or most painfully, "I'm taking Joshua with me." I still hear and see you pray for our family. You've not wavered in looking to God to carry you through this difficult *transformation. You don't have me all to yourself as you did when Justin went away for a weekend. And now, our joyful little Prince Joshua demands even more of my attention. I appreciate seeing that you haven't given up the fight for our oneness. I appreciate your continued commitment to look to the Lord for guidance. I appreciate you expressing what is deep inside your heart through cards and special gifts. I appreciate your passionate lovemaking and holding me close afterward to bask in the glow. I appreciate your smile, your flirting, and your gentle touch.*

Our differences have been present from the beginning. I've always said, "You balance me so well." Your strength is my weakness, and my strength is your weakness. These differences have helped me to grow spiritually. My patience has increased, my capacity to love is deeper, and my ability to love unconditionally is greater.

I will commit to loving God and you more by being obedient to reading and studying His Word more. Even to the extent to which I was able to do so before we were married. I will commit to a more purposeful and closer prayer relationship with God. I will read traditional and spiritual wedding vows to you with fresh light, deeper understanding, and a new zeal to commit each one to heart.

Life continues to happen to us and around us, reshaping

our marriage and even our vision of how we thought it would become. That is the beauty of God. The ways in which we respond to those changes is the beauty of our love. Since both God and love are beautiful, I commit to both in our marriage with great expectation for things to come. With all my heartfelt blessing.

Your wife, Naomi

To my dearest wife Naomi,

2-14-09

I am writing this letter to let you know, from the beginning of our relationship in marriage, it had to be ordained by God. Your relationship with God, time spent with family, your affection and love for others, and your ability to communicate with others, were the qualities I admired most in you.

The more God opened my eyes and truly my heart, I could see you were a jewel worth cherishing forever. I have appreciated the special qualities you have shown in ministering not only in word, but also in deed; the support you show when I make decisions for our family and the trust you have in me; and the ability you have in organizing the things in our home and lives.

Even in the worst of times, I have grown both spiritually and emotionally because of you. I have learned that without the fruit of the Spirit, it would have been impossible for me to love you like I do. And, even in the worst of times, my love still longs for you—your smile (wow), your kiss, and your special touch.

Beloved, God has truly ordained this marriage in heaven, long before it took place. This oneness He placed in us, through His son Jesus, is greater than what the world has to offer. I have learned this weekend to remember that there is nothing greater than a husband and wife together, sold out for Jesus, and leading the family to greatness.

United together in love for God's greater purpose can only lead to a more unified marriage and relationship. To love you unconditionally is truly a gift from God far beyond my imagination.

So, my dearest Naomi, as I close out this letter, please note, I will be committed to loving God and you more, by discerning His voice more in prayer, and spending more time in His Word so that my heart will still long and cherish the jewel God has given me in you.

Your loving husband, Kelvin

I prepared a copy of the traditional wedding vow, and an old anglican vow of spiritual commitment, which we recited. The latter reads as follows, and was based on 1 Corinthians 7:3:

> With my body, I thee worship
> My body will adore you, and
> Your body alone will I cherish.
> I will, with my body, declare your worth
> Let the husband render unto the wife due
> benevolence: and likewise, also the wife
> unto the husband.

With those being shared, we savored a reserved Valentine's Day dinner at Lebbie Lebkicher's at the Hershey Lodge. From lobster bisque to bananas Foster and chocolate fondue for two, we were enchanted with each other's company. Afterward, we drove fifteen miles to see the great jazz pianist, Steve Rudolph, and his band at the Hilton Harrisburg. Oh, how we enjoy jazz music! Kelvin and I sipped on mixed fruit beverages, snapped our fingers, and twisted our hips while shuffling our feet. We swayed to the smooth sounds of the night. Ah, we had a glow that outshined all the other lovebirds and Saturday nightclubbers. We were strengthening our marriage and celebrating new life developing in my womb. Yes, a weekend to remember!

Sunday's sessions began with "Woman to Woman: Embracing God's Wonderful Design" or "Man to Man: Stepping Up to a Higher Call," followed by "How Marriages Thrive," and finally, "Leaving a Legacy." As the conference neared closing, each couple was handed a cream-colored, heavyweight piece of paper printed with:

Our Marriage Covenant

Believing that God, in His wisdom and
providence,
Has established marriage as a covenant
relationship between one
man, and one woman, a sacred and lifelong
promise, reflecting our
unconditional love for one another and
believing that God intends for
the marriage covenant to reflect His promise to
never leave us nor forsake us.

*We, the undersigned, do hereby reaffirm
our solemn pledge to fulfill our marriage vows.*

Furthermore, we pledge to exalt the sacred

nature and permanence of the marriage covenant by calling others to honor and fulfill their marriage vows.

In the presence of God
And these witnesses, and by a holy covenant,

I, *Kelvin,* joyfully receive you as God's perfect gift for me to have and to hold from this day forward, for better, for worse, for richer, for poorer, in sickness and in health, to love you, to honor you, to *cherish* you and *protect* you, forsaking all others as long as we both shall live.

I, *Naomi,* joyfully receive you as God's perfect gift for me to have and to hold from this day forward, for better, for worse, for richer, for poorer, in sickness and in health, to love you, to honor you, to *respect* you and *submit* to you, forsaking all others as long as we both shall live.

Unless the Lord builds the house,
they labor in vain who build it
Psalm 127:1a

With the softness of his manly hands, he wiped the tears that streamed down my face as we, without hesitation, recited after the leader.

We returned home renewed, rejuvenated, and re-fueled, ready for whatever the enemy had planned to challenge our marriage. We each chose to receive our spouse as God's perfect provision for us. What a mighty God we serve!

On February 19, I had my first prenatal visit with Dr. Godorecci. A transabdominal ultrasound confirmed I was eight weeks, and four days pregnant, with a due date of September 26. Because of my age, I was considered high-risk and was scheduled with the Antenatal Testing Unit (ATU) on March 15 for a twelve-week examination. I left the office beaming from ear to ear with a "pregnancy glow." God had favored me once again, and I knew He was going to bless us with a daughter. The pregnancy had been met with minimal morning sickness. It was all I could do to keep from sharing the news with family, friends, and coworkers. After all, we got the usual "Hey, when are you guys having another baby?" "Joshua's walking now. You know what they say, 'He's moving out of the way for the next one.'" "When are you trying for that girl?" Not to mention, two of my very close cousins had announced their pregnancies. One was due at the end of June; the other, the end of July. Now I, the end of September. How exciting! Nonetheless, Kelvin and I decided to wait until the end of the first trimester before sharing the news.

One evening after work while I was lying in bed, "Hey babe—pray for our baby."

"Why? What's wrong?"

"I don't know. Something just doesn't feel right. I'm lying here beneath sheets, with my pajamas and bathrobe on, and I'm still cold. I feel chilled to my bones. I cannot seem to get warm. Just pray for our baby." My pediatrician mind wandered and pondered all that could have been wrong with our baby. "Now, Naomi, you have got to stop," I told myself. "God has everything under control. He planted this seed in my womb and knows the plans He has for it, and me. God, You can do anything but fail. Take control of my wandering thoughts and bring them under Your complete submission. Give me peace and rest this night. In Jesus's name, Amen."

Bishop Evans began a sermon series, Divine Stimulus Package: Miracles in March. God was going to intervene, override, and intercede on my behalf. There is a heavenly stimulus package available to me as a believer, which supersedes any government plan. When I stimulate Him in prayerful conversation and relationship, He stimulates faith, anointing, and power in my life. When I become acquainted with the significance of time in God's Word, I realize I dwell simultaneously in two dimensions: the natural and the supernatural. I am in the world but not of the world. I must recognize the difference between Chronos and Kairos. Chronos is man's time. It is chronological and quantitative. Kairos is the appointed time in God's purpose, the season of God, and is qualitative. Chronos is fleeting and waits for no one. It is out of our control. What makes it significant? Events, milestones, accomplishments. Kairos is that which pushes out time. It is where God dwells. It is from where He observes time. What makes it significant? God.

Saturday, March 7, I went to the braiding salon. Sitting in the chair, I thought I was spotting. After several hours, and having returned home, I realized I was. I became very concerned. After all, I never spotted with the two prior pregnancies. "Okay, Lord. I'm going to be optimistic. You know what this means. This is a new experience for me. My body needs to hold on to this pregnancy. Perhaps

I just need to lay down and rest." I shared my concerns with Kelvin. He was encouraging, supportive, and reassuring. After much prayerful thought, I developed a plan: I was going to church Sunday at eleven o'clock. If I was still spotting at the end of service, I would go to the emergency room for an evaluation.

As usual, Kelvin attended the eight o'clock service. The boys and I arrived at eleven to find him upstairs in the Children's Church.

"How are things?" he asked.

"Still spotting," I said with a phony smile across my face. "I am going to the emergency room if I'm still spotting after service."

"Don't worry," he said. "Everything is going to be all right. You'll see."

I signed Justin into Teen Church and brought Joshua along into the sanctuary. Sitting next to my girlfriend Tiffany, I pretended to enjoy service and wanted so badly to share my feelings. I desperately tried to enter a spirit of praise and worship. I participated in the morning prayer, sang along with the choir, and followed the reading of God's Word. Yet, my thoughts were with our baby. I prayed earnestly that all would be well.

That day's sermon was "Lord, grant me favor." My

external circumstances are not the primary validation that God is real in my life. His realization is manifested while I am going through trials. Just because I am in a valley, does not mean God is not with me. He is very present. The sermon included Psalm 5:11-12: "But let all who take refuge in you be glad; let them ever sing for joy. Spread your protection over them, that those who love your name may rejoice in you. Surely, Lord, you bless the righteous; you surround them with your favor as with a shield." When God's presence is real to you, there is no place you will ever go without being surrounded by His favor.

I anxiously fashioned my way to the ladies' room following service. Much to my dismay, I was still spotting. I remained in the stall, conversing with myself. "Okay, it's time to pull yourself together and go to the ER to be evaluated. This is probably no more than the first trimester spotting many women experience. Just because it is a first for you, does not mean you are losing the baby." I lingered long enough for the late parishioners to thin out. I went up to the Children's Church to relay the news to Kelvin. He grabbed and hugged me tightly for a long time in the middle of the hallway.

Again, he offered words of encouragement. "Don't worry. Everything is going to be all right."

Lifting my head and stepping back, I no longer wanted to be stoic and naïve. I wanted to be realistic. Looking him in the eyes, I said, "No, it's not. I'm losing our baby."

"Don't say that. Why would you say that?"

"Because it's true. There is no other reason for me to be spotting. I never saw any blood with the other pregnancies. Not one speck." Still holding on to a glimmer of hope, I declared, "I want to go alone. You take the boys and I will meet you at home when I am done. I should only be a few hours. I'll call with any changes and notify you when I'm done." I kissed him and left.

By that time, my functioning capacity was 85 percent physician, 15 percent pregnant woman. Walking briskly to the car, I pondered reasons why I could be spotting. No one knew I was pregnant. I could not call anyone for moral support. I needed to control this situation. I did not want to reveal my pregnancy through a threatened miscarriage. Who could I call? Oh, my sister-friend Gail. She's an obstetrician! After dialing her number, it went to voicemail. With as calm a spirit as possible, I left a voice message: "Hey Gail, it's Naomi. I hope your Sunday is well and you enjoyed service this morning. But, with all your busyness, you may even be on-call. Quick question. What are the possible reasons for late first trimester bleeding besides miscarriage? Whenever you can, no rush, just give me a callback. Thanks. Love ya!" Well, that was a start—not so helpful, but a start. I reached the car and got in. Sitting in the driver's seat, I prayed to my heavenly Father: "please save our baby." I questioned the All-Knowing One as to why I could be spotting. Then I flipped the equation to 85 percent pregnant woman, 15 percent physician and drove toward the hospital.

I signed into Virtua Health System Emergency Department, Voorhees Division, on Sunday, March 8, 2009, at 2:40 p.m. with the chief complaint: eleven weeks pregnant/vaginal bleeding, and was triaged as level 3-urgent. The waiting room was unusually filled, especially with pediatric patients. I was not present as a physician, but as a patient. I was handed a cup to provide a urine sample. When I went to collect it, the blood was bright red and moderate. My heart began to throb, and I began to sweat. For the first time, I understood the reality of my condition. With tear-filled eyes, I provided the sample and asked for a sanitary napkin. By then, it was four o'clock, and I had not received a call from Gail. I did not want to panic. Perhaps this was still spotting and I needed to be placed on bed rest. I had not been called to see a physician but was desperate to converse with one. I called my sister-friend Stephanie. She was a family practitioner. She answered the phone.

Tears flowed freely as I methodically presented my case. I closed my eyes as the words of her gentle, encouraging, professional voice spoke candidly to my situation, and heart. My breathing became increasingly erratic as I tried to maintain composure. Other patients were watching. After about an hour, I was able to share my case when Gail returned my call. When I completed that call, it was after seven p.m. I had been waiting four hours. The shifts changed, and one of the new nurses recognized my name on the board as one of the current staff pediatricians who used to moonlight in the ED. She saw the reason for my visit and that I was visibly and emotionally shaken. She took me from the general waiting area to a section behind the triage room and offered me water. She apologized for my long wait. But there had been so many pediatric patients, and the adult physicians had to help the pediatricians, thereby causing the adult patients to wait an unusually long time. It was from behind that triage room I called my husband. With a shaken voice and tears in my eyes, I told him I was pretty sure I was losing our baby and that I needed him to be with me. I wanted to inform my mother, so she could sit with the boys.

"Mommie, I do not have time to explain, and I do not want you to ask a lot of questions. Are you at Mum-Mum's?"

"Yes."

"Is everyone sitting around you?"

"Yes, I am at the dining room table. Everyone is here. Why?"

"I know you do not know this, but I am eleven weeks pregnant. I am sitting in the emergency department at Virtua Voorhees and I'm pretty sure I'm having a miscarriage. I need you to go to my house and sit with the boys, so Kelvin can come be with me. Just tell everyone you must leave, but do not tell them why. No one knows I am pregnant."

"What? Are you sure?"

"Yes, I am sure. I will fill you in on the details when I get home. I have been here four hours and still have not been called to the back. I want Kelvin to be here when they take me to do the ultrasound."

"Okay, Naomi. I'm leaving now. I'll be there as soon as I can."

Solemn, I replied, "Thank you."

Within an hour of being recognized by the nurse, I was called to the back. Kelvin had not yet arrived, but because of the long wait, the doctor wanted me taken to Radiology for an ultrasound immediately. Now, my pain was on a scale of four out of ten, and the bleeding was more like when I was having a menstrual cycle. The ultrasound technician was quite soothing. While performing a transabdominal, followed by a transvaginal scan, we talked about her family and children, a few current events, and my work as a pediatrician. She asked how far along I was and if I had any other children.

"I am eleven weeks and have three sons; two by birth and one by marriage. We are praying this one will be our girl. I guess it's too early for you to determine that, huh?"

"Well, no. You're right. I can't quite tell that information," she informed.

I knew full well she could not reveal that information, even if it had been as clear as day. I imagined my mouth was revealing what was deep within my heart. "I don't hear a heartbeat."

"Oh, that's because I don't have the sound turned on," she explained. "Well, it looks like we are all done here. I'll get you cleaned up, so you can go back to your room. Good luck with everything."

"Thank you. And… thanks for having such a calm spirit. You made me feel so much better."

"You're welcome." She smiled as I was taken to my room.

When I returned, Kelvin was waiting. Boy, was I glad to see him. We greeted each other with a kiss and embraced tightly. "The ultrasound technician did not seem as if anything were wrong with the baby. I guess I will be discharged home on bed rest for a few days." As I was speaking, the attending physician came in. She introduced herself and asked for a history.

After a short dialogue, she informed, "I'm sorry, but the baby is not there."

My heart dropped to the floor, and I began sobbing and hyperventilating. "What do you mean, the baby is not there?'"

"The ultrasound is not showing there is a baby," she repeated.

"I do not understand. I have been spotting since yesterday and only started bleeding more heavily since arriving here. I know I did not pass an embryo. How can you say the baby is not there?"

She clarified: "There is fetal tissue present, but not one the size you say you are. They are calling it a 'blighted ovum.' I am going to call your OB now. I will be right back."

Kelvin and I shared another private embrace as he comforted my breaking spirit. I did not understand. I had so many questions. I didn't ever recall hearing *blighted ovum* in all my years of training and practice.

"I spoke to Dr. Adamson," the doctor said upon her return. "Because you are stable, and do not have heavy bleeding, she wants you to follow up with her at eight thirty tomorrow morning."

I asked for a copy of the ultrasound along with my discharge papers. I was discharged at 10:07 p.m. with the diagnosis, "threatened abortion."

We arrived home and shared the details with my mother and Justin. Then I placed difficult phone calls to my mother-in-law, father, stepmother, and brother, trying to make sense of it all. I had not the strength to inform any others. My husband and mother would inform the remainder of the family.

Sobbing, I called my boss and asked him to only reveal my condition to our office manager. I had not told anyone that I worked with that I was pregnant and did not want them to know now.

With the deepest empathy he said, "Oh, Naomi. I am so sorry. But I think we all figured out you were pregnant anyway."

"That may be true, but I never confirmed it. Please, I will be out for at least one week; I do not want anyone to know." He obliged.

As the hour drew late, my mother went home and we all went to bed. Although uncertain of what to expect in the morning, I convinced Kelvin I would be fine to see Dr. Adamson alone. He could go to work and I would apprise him of the details. He held me close in his arms as I began to mourn the loss of our unborn child quietly. We fell asleep in each other's comfort.

Kelvin left for work at five fifteen a.m.; and Justin, to the bus stop by seven. After dropping Joshua off at daycare, I arrived at Dr. Adamson's office stoic but tearful. I signed in and took a seat among a few other patients. As emotions overwhelmed me, I was immediately taken to the back. Following a detailed history, physical exam, and review of the emergency department record, inclusive of ultrasound, she explained, "Based on the date of your last menstrual period, you are ten weeks, six days pregnant. However, the ultrasound reveals an eight-week irregular yolk sac and no fetal pole. Your baby stopped growing at that time. You will need to have a procedure to remove the baby. I cannot perform it today because you do not have anyone to drive you home. Your cervical opening is closed and you are not actively bleeding. You will be scheduled for suction dilatation and evacuation tomorrow morning." I was given a plastic container with instructions to collect any tissue I passed, in case it was the baby. "Rinse it with sterile saline and bring it with you tomorrow morning. If the bleeding or pain is severe, go to the emergency department." I took the container, and in disbelief, left.

Since Kelvin worked in a prison, I was not able to call and relay the news. I drove home in a daze, attempting to manage the *what-ifs*, *whys*, and *what am I going to dos* that were flooding my mind. I just wanted to be home alone with my thoughts.

I laid in my bed and drifted between crying, praying, waiting, wondering, and sleeping. After a couple of hours, the pain hit me. At first, it was mild, but it soon progressed to moderate, with cramping and bleeding. I was terrified. I called my mother, who had experienced two miscarriages thirty-five years prior. I remembered talking to her about them decades ago, and right now, I needed my mother. I knew my body was attempting to release my unborn child. The reality of it was more than I could bear. My mother's words were compassionate, empathetic, and heartfelt. She knew *exactly* what I was experiencing—the physical and emotional pain. There was no one in the world I would rather be talking with. Several times over the next four hours, I called her, weeping and wailing in agonized mourning. "It really hurts, Mommie. Is it supposed to hurt this badly? I'm losing my baby! I'm losing my baby! I don't know what to do." As the pain intensified, I passed tissue from my body. I collected it several times as instructed, each time terrified that I would be retrieving my baby from the toilet.

Kelvin called on his way home and was disappointed I opted to go to the doctor's appointment alone. He could have been there to support me through this most difficult time. But the truth of the matter is, I wanted—I *needed*—to experience this alone. I needed to be alone with God and my baby. I needed time to talk to Him, and her, through this very personal and cathartic experience. This child Kelvin and I so desperately wanted, the one we prayed would be our daughter, was leaving my body. She belonged to the Lord, as with prior pregnancies, and she had been given over to Him from the moment I became aware of conception. When Kelvin arrived, he prayed, comforted, and embraced me, but not before presenting me with a bouquet of red roses.

On Tuesday, March 10, I awoke nauseous as I

thought of the impending procedure. I retrieved the refrigerated container labeled "Products of Conception" and somberly went to the car. I sat in silence as my husband prayed and then drove us to the surgical center. The staff were all kind. I was quickly and efficiently processed and prepped. I heard over and over: "Mrs. Hugh, I'm so sorry for your loss." Dr. Adamson expressed her condolences, and the anesthesiologist administered IV-conscious sedation (to help me relax and block the pain of the procedure) . After a paracervical blockade (an anesthetic procedure), I underwent suction dilation and evacuation for a blighted ovum and incomplete spontaneous abortion. The products of conception were sent to pathology, and for chromosome analysis. I tolerated the procedure well, with minimum blood loss, and was transferred to the recovery room. Again: "Mrs. Hugh, I'm so sorry for your loss." Once I was stable, I sobbed and embraced my waiting husband.This was my inauguration day.

DEVOTIONAL ANECDOTE:

A LESSON FROM HANNAH

†

The story of Hannah is one of grace, favor, and courage.

1 Samuel 1:1-28; 2:21 Hannah was the first wife of Elkanah. After they had been married for ten years, he also married Peninnah because of Hannah's barrenness. Peninnah bore him sons and daughters.

Once a year, Elkanah and his wives went out of the city to worship and sacrifice unto the Lord in Shiloh. Elkanah gave portions to Peninnah and her children. But to Hannah he gave a double portion because the Lord had shut up her womb. Peninnah provoked Hannah painfully to make her worry, grieve, and stop eating. Elkanah asked, "Why do you cry? Why do you not eat? Why is your heart grieved? Am I not better than ten sons?"

On one of these yearly visits to Shiloh, Hannah went before the High Priest alone. Her soul was bitter.

In the sanctuary before the Lord, she prayed and wept agonizingly. She vowed [to the Lord]: If You look upon my affliction, remember me, and forget me not, but will give me a man child, then I will give him unto You all the days of his life, and no razor shall come to his head. She spoke in her heart and only her lips moved. Her voice was not heard. Therefore, Eli thought she was drunk, condemned her conduct, and commanded that she put away her wine. She explained, "No, I am a woman of a sorrowful spirit. I am not drunk. I have poured out my soul before the Lord. Do not accuse me of being a wicked woman. Out of the abundance of my complaint and grief have I spoken unto you, Lord." He charged her to go in peace, and the God of Israel grant her the petition that she asked of Him. She asked for allowance to find grace in His sight. She left and ate, and her countenance was no longer sad.

Hannah and her husband rose up early the next morning, worshipped before the Lord, and then returned home. Elkanah knew Hannah his wife, and the Lord remembered her. Before the year was up, she conceived and bore a son. In grateful memory of the Lord's favor, she named him Samuel, because she had asked of God.

Hannah did not return to Shiloh to worship and

sacrifice until Samuel was weaned [likely three years]. When he was, she went up with him, her husband, and their offerings. She entered the house of the Lord and reminded Eli the High Priest, that she was the woman who had stood and prayed. "I prayed for this child and the Lord has given me my petition. Therefore, I have also granted him to the Lord for as long as he lives."

She offered a prayer of thanksgiving. "My heart rejoices in the Lord. My horn is exalted in the Lord. My mouth boasts over my enemies for I delight in Your deliverance. There is no one holy like the Lord, no one besides You, no rock like our God. Do not continue to speak proudly and arrogantly. God knows and will weigh your deeds. The bows of the warrior are broken, but those who stumble are armed with strength. The well-fed are begging for food while the hungry are satisfied. She who was barren has born seven children, but she who has many is bereaved. The Lord brings death and makes alive. He sends poverty and wealth; He humbles and exalts. He raises the poor from the dust and the needy from the ash heap. He seats them with princes and has them inherit a throne of honor. The foundations of the earth are His and upon them He has set the world. He will guard the feet of His faithful servants, but the wicked will be silenced in the place of darkness. It is not by strength that one prevails. Those who oppose the Lord will be broken. The Most High will thunder from heaven. The Lord will judge the ends of the earth. He will give strength to His king and exalt the horns of the anointed."

Then Elkanah went home, but Samuel ministered before the Lord under Eli the High Priest. After Samuel, Hannah had three sons and two daughters.

Hannah's desire for a son was not merely maternal. She wanted a son who would one day change the nation. She wanted him to be a man after God's own heart, to be a future prophet, priest, or king. She had prayed for the impossible; though barren, she would nevertheless conceive. A feat when actualized would clearly mean that God would be glorified.

"When God gives you a promise, you essentially become pregnant with it. If you plan to carry the promise to full term, you must travail " (Grady 2012, 92).

I prayed for a daughter. God had proven to me that He had honored our sacrifice of abstinence before marriage when He blessed us with Joshua. Certainly, He was pleased with our godly union and would bless my womb with His female child. I dedicated her life to Him from the time I learned of her conception. We were prepared to be responsible stewards of her life. She would be raised to become His kingdom heir.

But the Lord gives, and He takes away.

Pray, even in your weakest moments. "That is why, for Christ's sake, I delight in weaknesses, in insults, in hardships, in persecutions, in difficulties. For when I am weak, then I am strong" (2 Corinthians 12:10 NIV).

QUESTIONS TO CONSIDER

1. Who or what is your Peninnah?
2. How is she taunting you?
3. What petition has God granted that you have not dedicated back to Him?
4. What dream have you carried that has been prematurely lost from your womb?

WORDS OF ENCOURAGEMENT

Do not let the voice of Peninnah speak louder than your faith in God

SONG FOR YOUR SEASON

"He Will Take the Pain Away"—Kirk Franklin

ACT OF KINDNESS

Write yourself a letter. In it, permit yourself to grieve a loss you've not yet accepted.

CHAPTER THREE

†

Letting Go

D r. Adamson suggested I remain home for two
weeks—the first for physical recovery; the second, emotional. I did not think I could bear
mourning the loss of our baby, alone, for two weeks. So
I opted to remain for one. Again, I asked my husband to
respect my wishes for privacy. Justin went to school, and
I took Joshua to day care. I needed only the morning and
early afternoon to process my feelings. Justin would be
home by two thirty p.m., and Kelvin an hour later. Then
I could appreciate the company of my family.

I spent much of the time talking to God. After all, I
had learned to trust His sovereignty, walk by faith, seek
His direction, and rely on His promises. What I needed
to understand was: Why? Not the why of "How could
you allow this to happen?" But the why of "What are
you trying to teach me?" No circumstance was ever
wasted. There was a lesson to be learned through every
triumph and every trial. I cried, prayed, read Scripture,

and listened to inspirational music. In between, I allowed my mind to wonder about the what-ifs. Did we lose Jeremiah Benjamin or Bethany Emille? Would I finally have birthed the daughter who my heart desired for so long? Or would I have continued to boast of my boys and me? Would this pregnancy have been as delightful as the others? Would it have been impossible to contain the pregnancy glow? Would my body have again swollen to the point of needing to wear my wedding rings on a chain around my neck? How would Joshua have responded to my growing belly? Would Kelvin's smile have radiated at the sight of his heir growing inside my womb? Would he have enjoyed lying on the bed, feeling his seed move about and stretch my skin? Would he have rushed to slip on my shoes when I could no longer see my feet? Would he and Justin have looked at each other in disbelief and said "September 26," when I commenced to cry for no good reason? Would Kelvin have been able to videotape this baby's birth? Would we have found enough words to thank God for the blessing of another precious gift of life? While these questions brought me great joy, the reality of their denial brought me great anguish. My womb was empty, my heart was aching, and my mind was exhausted.

Justin's presence after school delighted my spirit and

afforded us the necessary mother-child bonding time. One day, he asked without fully understanding, "So, there's really no baby in there anymore?"

"No. There's really not."

Every so often, when I was overcome with emotion, he hugged me tight and said, "Mommie, I'm really sorry you have to go through this."

Later, Kelvin came home and handed me a yellow index card with the following handwritten on it:

Naomi
<u>Scriptures to Read</u>
Deuteronomy 28:1–14
Psalms 91
The Book of John

<u>Faith Scriptures</u>
Genesis
Chapters 12, 15, 17, 18, 22 & 24
Hebrews Chapter 11

He prayed for me, us, and our family. He continued to show compassion, and strength, and he maintained headship of our home.

Returning to work the following week was more difficult than anticipated. Examining children, especially babies, was overwhelming. I found myself remaining in the exam room, sobbing in between examining patients. And seeing the pregnant belly of my office assistant, who was due the same month as I had been, was even more difficult. She had a very different perspective about her pregnancy. She was half my age, and hers was unexpected. Her prevailing statement: "My life is in shambles!" There was a void in my heart and heaviness in my spirit; nevertheless, I thanked God for hiding His Word in my heart so I might encourage her to the contrary. "Children are a heritage of the Lord, and the fruit of the womb is His reward. He will never give you more than you can bear. Don't look to man to be your provider. Your God will supply all your needs according to His riches in glory by Christ Jesus. God has a purpose and plan for your life. Seek Him and He will reveal it to you. Trust Him, He will direct your path (Psalms 127:3; 1 Corinthians 10:13; Philippians 4:19; Jeremiah 29:11; Proverbs 3:5–6)." Isn't it funny—when you share God's Word to bless others, you receive a blessing in return?

My office manager, Lynne, was the only one, aside from Dr. Mohazzebi, who knew of my loss. She was very gracious and discretely attentive to my needs during the transitional period.

I went to see Dr. Adamson on March 23, two weeks after the procedure. I was recovering as expected. She had not received the results of the pathology or chromosomal analysis. The reason for my loss remained unknown. However, I was informed of good news: after two menstrual cycles, we could begin planning our next pregnancy.

The days turned into weeks, and my heart began to heal. My three sister-friends—Gail, Stephanie, and Lynda—were a source of great comfort and encouragement. Though they had not experienced such a loss, their support was tremendously appreciated. While at work, on Wednesday, April 22, I received a voice message on my cell phone to call Dr. Adamson. I went into a private room and shut the door. This was it. This was the moment I'd been waiting for. My heart began to race and my palms began to sweat. I felt a bit queasy. I whispered a prayer for God to prepare and quiet my heart. When I returned the call, she asked about my general well-being, and we exchanged customary pleasantries. Then she said, "I have the results of the chromosomal analysis. It's 47 XX plus 7."

XX? I thought. *That's a girl!* "Okay. Thank you for

letting me know." I hung up the phone. The tears streamed down my face. It was a girl. I lost my girl. My daughter. My Bethany. I cried aloud. "Lord, thank You for my Bethany. Thank You for allowing me to experience her presence for eleven weeks. Thank You for giving her life. Thank You for creating her whole and complete in You. Thank You for the joy of knowing I will see her again. Thank You for giving me a daughter, for fulfilling my heart's desire. Thank You for the ability to dream, to imagine, to see her in my mind's eye. Now, God, settle my heart. Turn my tears of sorrow into tears of unspeakable joy. Give me peace. Steady my mind. Control my thoughts. I have to work until eight p.m. My patients need me. Be my strength in the midst of weakness. I need You now. In Jesus's name, Amen."

I spent the next day researching nonmosaic trisomy 7. (This is what Dr. Adamson meant when she said 47XX plus 7. This is a chromosomal abnormality in which every cell of the body has an extra copy of chromosome number 7. It is thought to result in spontaneous abortion during the first trimester in most conceptions. The mosaic form is nonlethal). As a pediatrician, I had no recollection of any patient with this condition. What would my daughter have experienced had she lived? Could I have handled her physical and mental health challenges? What would have been her quality of life? What would have been her life expectancy? How would she have changed my life for the better? Would we have appreciated the depths of our love simply by gazing into our eyes? I had so many questions and few answers. There were no known nonmosaic Trisomy 7s that resulted in live births. Therefore, my heart was content in knowing that, Bethany was created for His divine purpose. I will spend the rest of my life awaiting its revealing.

For the next two months, Kelvin and I focused on the love we had for each other and our children. I longed for a way to thank my sister-friends for being so supportive. I purchased silver, chain-link toggle bracelets, each with a dangling heart charm that was inscribed with "Sister Friend," and presented them in steel blue boxes. On pastel-colored index cards, I wrote "47 XX + 7," and tucked them inside individually selected Mother's Day cards. That's it. Happy Mother's Day to my beautiful sister-friends.

My second menstrual cycle ended on our third wedding anniversary. It could not have happened more perfectly. My mother-in-law gifted us an overnight stay at a hotel in Atlantic City the following weekend. Justin and Joshua would stay with my mother. It was exactly what our marriage needed. "Two are better than one and a threefold cord is not quickly broken" (Ecclesiastes 4:9–12). As God would have it, we were favored with a room upgrade upon check-in. We felt like giddy newlyweds, and Kelvin carried me over the threshold of our suite for the night. The view of the city lights overlooking the marina was lovely. The bathroom was deluxe and included complementary plush white cotton robes and slippers. The refrigerator was stocked with personal-sized bottles of top-shelf spirits, soft drinks, and water. And the bed was king-size, with luxurious white linens, calling for us to partake in sensual indulgence. Yes, we were poised to celebrate our marriage union and planning our next pregnancy.

Kelvin changed into a plaid black-and-white sports jacket, white shirt, black pants, and black shoes. I, into a knee-length red dress with jeweled silver embellishments along the length of an empire waistline, and silver shoes with straps. We felt absolutely blessed as we walked hand in hand around the hotel, marveling at the beauty of its artistic design, meandering in and out of high-end shops, being photographed in front of waterfalls and glass sculptures, and dining at a seafood buffet. Earth Wind & Fire was the main concert hall entertainment. Unfortunately, the only seats available were front row and priced out of our financial stewardship zone. Instead, we enjoyed the comedy show in the secondary auditorium; those tickets were complementary with our upgrade at check-in. Our evening was spent smitten in each other's company, the night engulfed in intimacy.

Thank You, Lord, for allowing us to celebrate another year of marriage. You have blessed our lives with Joshua and our hearts with Bethany. Our deepest desire is to bear another. Our union is meant to worship You. Consecrate our time. Be in the midst. Plant the seed again. Grant us the opportunity to steward another angel, in Jesus's name, Amen.

Following a breakfast fit for royalty, we shopped at nearby outlets, relaxed on the beach, soaked in the warmth of the June sun, and watched the roaring waves of the Atlantic Ocean lap gently on the edge of the sandy shore. The smell of salt water and the sound of seagulls amid happy beachgoers satisfied our hearts. We strolled the boardwalk from Arkansas Avenue to Steel Pier amusement park, appreciating the sights, sounds, and smells along the way. What a wonderful time of sharing. We opted for a pushcart ride back down the boardwalk to the Pier at Caesars. Our cart operator was a young international student working in America for the summer. We thanked God for our paths meeting as he shared his amazing story during the ride. We tipped him a double portion and entered the Pier for dinner.

It had been only twenty-four hours but it'd seemed longer. The time spent was needed therapy for our marriage. Loving without restriction is liberating. We looked forward to next month, to eight beautiful days in Playa del Carmen, Mexico. God is the god of restoration and increase. We believed Him for both.

It was July 2, and we were due to leave for Mexico in one week. I was anxious and wanted to know if I was pregnant. So, there it went: I took the urine test, and there it was. Two lines! It's positive! We were pregnant again! We were overjoyed. The last time, our parents were disappointed we had not shared the news. With elation and discretion, this time I shared. Let the fireworks begin! After the holiday, I contacted Dr. Adamson, and she sent me in for a quantitative human chorionic gonadotrophin (HCG) serum pregnancy test. It was 175, which confirmed the pregnancy. However, the hormone level was low. It was very early in the pregnancy, but Dr. Adamson wanted to ensure the level was increasing. Since we were leaving for Mexico in two days' time, I opted to repeat the test the next day. It was 214.

July 8—what a way to begin a vacation, with new life developing inside. Our flight was early the next morning. Justin, in his mindless rebellion, had decided earlier he did not want to accompany us to Mexico. We planned for him to spend the week with my mother. It was ten thirty p.m., and I was preparing to drop him off. Before we left, I used the bathroom. To my horror, there was blood on the toilet paper. I flushed the toilet and, in an anxious panic, began to pray: "Oh, dear God, please. Not again." I focused on my stomach as I stared at my reflection in the mirror. Fighting back the tears, I gathered myself and left the bathroom. I looked at my husband but could not bear to tell him. Justin and I left, and I drove twenty minutes to my mother's house, all the while talking to God: "Please don't take this baby from my womb. My heart cannot take this pain again. Please, God. Stop the bleeding." When we arrived, I disappointedly shared the news with my mother, but not with Justin. I purposefully embraced and kissed him good-bye. I informed my mother, "We have eight hours before leaving for the airport. I'll call you in the morning with an update." She cried, hugged me tightly, then kissed me good-bye.

July 9—I awoke at four a.m., before Kelvin. Sitting on the toilet, I was still bleeding. My head was spinning, and my breathing was laborious. Clenching against the middle of my chest, my body began rocking back and forth. In silence, the tears began to flow. Pleading with God in prayer: "I cannot fathom this. Help me understand. Please do not call another baby from my womb. I am losing another baby. Please, God. Do not allow this again. Please. My heart cannot harbor this hurt again. Please, God. Please. How am I going to tell my husband?"

With a quiet whimper, I emerged from the bathroom, packing toiletries. Kelvin asked, "What's wrong? Why are you crying?"

"I have to pack these. I showed him a box of tampons and a bag of panty liners.

"Why do you need those?"

Sobbing, I replied, "I am losing the baby. I started bleeding last night, and it has not stopped."

He embraced me tightly and kissed my forehead. "Aww, really? Not again. I'm so sorry, Naomi. What are we going to do?"

"I will be fine. It's not like last time. I am early enough in the pregnancy; it will be like having a heavy period. We can still go on the trip. I just have to call everyone and tell them I'm losing another baby." Still sobbing.

Reassuringly, Kelvin said, "You don't have to tell anyone anything. We can go on our trip and have a good time. You can tell everyone when we get back." And we packed up the car and drove to the airport.

Have a good time? I'm losing another baby and you expect me to have a good time? That's a lot easier said than done. But, for the sake of our family vacation, I will try. I could not bear the weight of withholding the news until after the trip. We boarded the plane. As I fastened my seat belt, with Joshua snuggled in his blanket on my lap, I made the calls. Mommie, then my mother-in-law, Mom Anna. They offered heartfelt condolences, as the pain of their words was palpable through the phone. I called Daddy, and my step-sister answered the phone, "Hey, Miss Prego!" After a brief, pretentious conversation with her, I relayed the news to my father. Through tears, I asked him to tell Cris and Rasheeda, my step-mother, and -sister, respectively. I sat, quietly sobbing and looking out the window, waiting for takeoff. Grabbing my hand

and rubbing it gently, Kelvin soothed my weary soul with unspoken words. Thank God for the strength of the moment. Now, on to Mexico to heal.

We landed in Cancun and took a forty-five-minute van ride to Playa del Carmen. The Sandos Playacar was a sight for my sore eyes. A walk on the marbled floor, through the open-air lobby—with its vaulted ceilings and refreshingly warm cross breeze—was a welcoming experience. The cool blue waters of the winding pools, bridges, and fountains invited my body to swim. And the breathtaking view of a pale blue sky, flooded with billows of soft white clouds, opposed a horizon of crystal clear, blue-green water that beat against white sandy beaches that stretched as far as my eyes could see. It was the thing my weary heart desired. The hot sun warmed me to the core as I stood standing with my eyes closed, hands over-lapped atop my pelvis, asking God to heal my hurting heart. I promised Him I would not ask why. Rather: "Help me understand."

The first six days proved more challenging than expected. Although thrilled to be vacationing with fam-ily—swimming through underground river caves, dining with mariachi, shopping in the village, and relaxing by the pools—the stark reality remained: I was not merely menstruating. I was miscarrying. For six days, I vacillated between enjoying the occasion and mourning the moment. Kelvin could sense my ambivalence. For the next two days, I prayed God would turn my heart toward my husband. I apologized for my actions of seeming disinterested and, at times, to have short-tempered conversation. It affirmed the differences in our capacities to cope and process loss. All was not cast away. My ability to swoon—and his, to beguile—was delighted in after the sun set, when the stars twinkled in the night, and Joshua was sound asleep.

We returned to the States refreshed and ready for what God had in store. It was nearly August, and my cousins, who were expecting the same time as I had been, had delivered their babies—a boy near the end of June, and a girl five weeks later. Notwithstanding the agony of my own heart, I celebrated the joy of their blessings. I still trusted the Lord, again, for the fruit of my womb. And right then, we had a great reason to celebrate: Joshua was turning two! Our family went to mark the occasion at a local amusement and water park. Gladness filled my bosom as I watched my nearly fifteen-year-old splash about in the kiddie section with his two-year-old brother. My heart still longed for the day Joshua would be called "big brother."

I began tracking my cycle using ovulation kits and

noticed it lasting three rather than five days: it was time to consult Dr. Adamson. Because I was forty-two, with a recent history of two spontaneous first-trimester losses, and now, shortened menstrual cycles, I was referred to Dr. Louis Manara, a reproductive endocrinology and infertility specialist. The consultation was on Thursday, September 24. Following a successful workup and being informed of our insurance company's full infertility coverage, I shared with Kelvin Dr. Manara's assessment and plan of care. Even after seeking God, we were wavering regarding the decision. Was it unfaithful to pursue man's capacity to assist with what should be reserved for God's favor? We had *our three sons*. Wasn't that enough?

Yet, I care for many children who, had it not been for the assistance of an infertility specialist, would not have been given the gift of life. Should it be that the only ones to benefit from infertility treatments are those who have never conceived on their own? Kelvin and I honored God and sanctified our bodies before marriage. Was it unreasonable to desire God to bless our marriage with another child? Were we selfish? Ungrateful? After pondering these questions and considering their answers, we proceeded forward—I with great enthusiasm, Kelvin with cautious reservation.

The first cycle of transvaginal-ovarian ultrasounds and blood work began. This type of ultrasound is an imaging scan that doctors use to examine the inside of a person's pelvic region. They would be done early-morning and twice a week. By midmorning, I would receive a call with the results, and instruction for the evening. The use of a specific medication and its dose would be determined based on where I was in my cycle. Intercourse was freely enjoyable; however, there were nights when it was instructed and timed. In the beginning, those days were no different than any other. Admittedly, there were occasions when the day's responsibilities yielded nighttime fatigue, and fatigue led to frustration and resentment of the process. On October 23, pregnancy test number one: negative. LMP (last menstrual period) began October 25. *Okay, Lord, we're continuing to trust You.*

Second cycle. Each morning that I saw Dr. Manara, his demeanor and candor eased the anxiety hidden within my heart, despite this process challenging the core of Kelvin and my belief system and marriage. In the evenings, I would slip into the bathroom, retrieve the medication log, dial the dose, and inject that portion subcutaneously into my abdomen, praying, "not my will, but Thy will be done." Each time we had intercourse, we prayed for conception to occur. On November 18, pregnancy test number two: negative. LMP began November 19.

Third cycle.. Since medication, coupled with timed intercourse, had proven unsuccessful, the option of IUI (Intrauterine Insemination) was introduced. Because of the favorable results from November 25's ultrasound and labs, the IUI was set for November 27: Black Friday. Thanksgiving was significant and reflective. We thanked God for His continued blessings upon our family, and the hope of extending it into the future. The night was met with compassion, and the morning with enthusiasm. The sample was lovingly collected and taken to Dr. Manara's office. It was prepared, washed, and deemed acceptable. My uterus was inseminated without difficulty. I felt wonderfully hopeful! The next pregnancy test was planned for December 11. I left the office with a bright smile on my face and a confident prayer in my heart. *That's it, Lord. It's Your time to shine. Death and life are in the power of Your will. I am trusting You to work through Dr. Manara and bless my womb once again.* Two weeks passed, and LMP began December 10. On December 11, pregnancy test number three: negative.

With great disappointment and reservation, we

began the fourth cycle. Realizing we were already blessed parents, did we need to continue "trying to play God" to be so again? Perhaps He was speaking to us through each negative test. My heart and spirit had not discerned that as truth. *Please, Lord, speak to me audibly and clearly concerning Your will.*

December 10, 16, and 18 were positive visits. We were encouraged to move forward with a second IUI on December 21. Kelvin was challenged beyond his comfort zone as this would be an in-office specimen collection, while I would be at work. He arrived for his appointment with my photo and three years of marital thoughts. While in the collection room, he called. While talking, I flirted and enticed him to excitation. After he submitted his sample, Kelvin waited as the specimen was prepared. It was "very good," and he was cleared to leave. I traveled to the office during lunchtime for the insemination. Again, it was completed without difficulty. The next pregnancy test was scheduled for January 4, 2010. Knowing my husband had been there this morning, and I having just been inseminated with his seed, I left blushing like a bride of her wedding night. On the way back to work, I called Kelvin to inform him the procedure went well. He responded with assurance, "Naomi, I love you, but don't ever ask me to do that again." At that moment, I knew that would be our last cycle. No matter how promising future ultrasounds and labs would be, that was it.

Christmas and the New Year were met with much desire and reflection. We had begun 2009 with the excitement of fruit in the womb and endured the anguish of the loss of that fruit—twice. Alas, we found ourselves having come full circle, awaiting the result of a pregnancy test. Monday, January 4, pregnancy test number four: negative. My heart was broken. LMP began January 5. Despite the resolute conviction of my husband's words, I knew IVF (in vitro fertilization) was our last hope. I was content with pursuing this option.

Wednesday, January 6, 2010: the fifth cycle. Early morning, transvaginal-ovarian ultrasound, and labs followed. As soon as I reached work, I called MumMum to wish her a happy eighty-fifth birthday. I love her so, and looked forward to having another child as a branch off her family tree. We talked for a while. A smile spread across my face as my heart delighted in the goodness of God's keeping power. "Have a blessed day, MumMum. I love you" ended our conversation.

At eleven o'clock a.m. my cell phone rings. It's Dr.

Manara. I am surprised to hear his voice, and not that of an office assistant. He is calling to relay difficult news. My FSH (follicle stimulating hormone) had increased greatly from 16 to 24. My ovaries were not responsive. I had three options: increase gonadotrophin (medication), IVF, or egg donation. Increasing gonadotrophin may or may not stimulate the ovaries to produce eggs. He discouraged IVF (for reasons I could not grasp); instead, he suggested I have a healthy egg donated from a twenty-year-old woman, fertilized with my husband's sperm and then inserted into my womb. That child would not be genetically mine but offered the best chance of conception. "If you continue on your own, you have a less than ten percent chance of ever conceiving again."

My heart sank, and I was overcome with disbelief. The news was devastatingly unexpected. *Less than 10 percent chance of ever conceiving again?* It was one thing to *decide* not to have any more children, but quite another to be *told* you cannot. I needed time to process this information. Dr. Manara suggested I discuss the options with Kelvin and inform him of our decision. It was a difficult one. The doctor gave me the medication doses for the next five nights and scheduled an appointment for January 11. I hung up the phone, and once again, found myself weeping on a Wednesday.

Thursday, January 7, 2010: one-month shy of my forty-third birthday. Trusting God has been a way of life. I have always said, "I want to have five children." Why five? I do not know. It had been a lifelong desire of my heart. God, in His infinite wisdom, granted my desire. He never revealed the how; just fulfilled the desire. I had two sons by birth, one by marriage, one daughter in His bosom, and one other I will come to know by-and-by. That's five. The last two were as real to me as the tangible three. I experienced the joy of a positive pregnancy test, and the glow of knowing their seeds were in my womb. I thanked God for this most difficult process, and I was humbled by the invaluable lesson it had taught: letting go of what I wanted and appreciating what I had.

DEVOTIONAL ANECDOTE:

A LESSON FROM ANNA

✝

Anna's is a story of devotion and faithful encouragement.

Luke 2:36–38

Anna was a prophetess whose father was from the tribe of Asher. She had lived with her husband for only seven years before he died. Now, eighty-four, she never departed from the area of the temple and served God day and night with fastings and prayers. From the moment she saw and overheard Simeon pronounce a blessing while dedicating the baby Jesus, she gave thanks and never ceased speaking of Him to all those who were looking for a Redeemer in Jerusalem.

Anna was a Hebrew, and like her Old Testament parallel, Hannah, her name means "grace." She was gifted in proclaiming God's truth to, and encouraging, other believers. She is part of the believing remnant of Israel and is a living emblem of God's faithfulness to His people.

Her husband died seven years into their marriage, seemingly before she bore children. She lived as a widow until age eighty-four. We learned in Ruth that widows were social outcasts who lived in poverty and namelessness. That does not appear to be the case for Anna. Though she never remarried, she was either taken care of by the church or lived off her husband's riches. She devoted scores of years to temple worshipping, fasting, and praying.

Anna did not bury her hope with her husband. In place of what God took, He gave her more of Himself. Time with God healed her brokenness and made room for trustworthiness. She lived a life of godly self-control. Despite her loss, she learned to encourage others. For decades upon decades, she remained an example of devotion and faithful encouragement.

Unlike Anna, my womb experienced the gift of life. Like her, my heart experienced brokenness and made room for trustworthiness. I pray that as I grow old, it will be said of me that I devoted years to worship, fasting, and prayer, and scores were encouraged by my faithful devotion.

QUESTIONS TO CONSIDER

1. Name one thing God is calling you to let go?
2. What makes it difficult for you to let go?
3. Do you believe yourself to be a remnant of His faithfulness? Why or why not?
4. Despite a loss, to what have you remained devoted?

WORDS OF ENCOURAGEMENT

God's grace is given freely. There is nothing you can do to deserve it. There is nothing you can do to earn it. It is His goodwill to all. You need only open your heart to receive it.

A SONG FOR YOUR SEASON

"He's Been Faithful"—Brooklyn Tabernacle Choir

ACT OF KINDNESS

Stand in front of a mirror. Speaking directly to yourself, permit yourself to grieve whatever you lost.

†
Stop Running through the Woods

It was Tuesday, February 1, 2011. I was lying beside my husband, in a deep sleep, when the phone rang. He answered. Listening to the voice on the other end, he nudged me. "It's for you."

"Hello," I answered with a groggy voice.

"Is this Naomi Hill Hugh?" a male voice asked.

Heart sinking into my stomach . . .

"Yes, it is."

"This is Officer Blank from the Deptford Township Police Department. Do you own a white Mitsubishi Montero Sport?"

Heart racing. . .

"Yes."

"Do you know anyone who lives in Deptford?"

Breathing deeply . . .

"Yes, my mother."

"Your vehicle was left abandoned here," he declared.

Nauseous . . ."What? I don't understand. Where? What time is it?"

Sitting up . . ."Ma'am, it's two thirty in the morning," he explained.

This is not making sense. . . . ."My vehicle is parked in the driveway."

Holding my head . . ."No, ma'am. It's not. A young man was driving your vehicle across the bridge from Deptford into Woodbury. He made an illegal U-turn in the middle of the street, so a Woodbury officer pulled him over. When the officer approached the driver's side window, he took off. He was followed back across the bridge into Deptford, but was lost when he turned onto Highland Avenue then into Narraticon. Deptford PD was called for backup. We drove around and found the vehicle abandoned in the parking lot of Narraticon. Where does your mother live?"

Trembling, tears running down my cheeks, my nose running . . .

"She lives in the Woods at Narraticon," I reported.

Breathing laboriously . . .

"What's her name . . . address . . . phone number?"

Faster . . .

"I don't know. Wait a minute. I can't think. I can tell you how to get there from Highland Avenue."

My head is pounding. . . .

"My son must have taken my car," I said.

Oh dear Jesus . . .

"Your son? What's his name?" the officer asked.

My sweet Jesus . . .

"Justin . . . Justin Hill."

Cover my son, Jesus. . . .

"How old is he?"

"Sixteen."

Rocking back and forth . . .

"Does he have a gun?" he inquired.

Father God!

"A gun? No!" I proclaimed. "He doesn't have a gun!"

Send a legion of angles, right now, God!

"Are you sure?" he stressed."Yes, I'm sure!" I insisted.

"Then why did he run?" he asked, perplexed.

Palms sweating, pajamas wet . . .

"He ran because he's scared. He knows if he gets caught, he is going to jail. He has done this before. I can't believe he's done it again. I know he's scared. He's harmless. He's just scared. Please don't hurt my son!"

Agonizing moans . . .

"Do you think he went to your mother's apartment?"

Bewildered . . . "No, he would never do that. He would never involve her," I explained.

Tears pouring down . . . "We'll send an officer to check it out. If he calls or returns home, please, call the Deptford Township Police Department. The number is . . ."

Suffocating . . .

"Okay. Thank you."

Click.

All the while, Kelvin lay listening. Then: "Well, Justin has to come to terms with himself. He continues to do what he wants, when he wants, and thinks he can get away with it. Naomi, there's nothing else you can do. Just turn him over to God."

With tears staining my pillow, I lay down and prayed.

My cell phone rang; caller ID: Justin.

In desperation . . .

"Mom tell mhe you love mhe! I need to hear you say it! Mom, say it! Tell mhe you love mhe!"

"Justin, I love you! I love you! I LOVE YOU! Where are you?!"

"I'm in the woodz."

"What? The woods?!"

"Yez! The police are prolly gonna call the house. When they do, tell them you don't have a son and that someone stole your car."

"What? They already called. They asked about MiMom. I told them where she lived."

"I took ya car 'cause I wanted to go for a drive. I decided to drive out Woodbury. When I got across the bridge, I saw a cop sittin' there, parked on the side. I popped a U-turn and headed back to Deptford. I saw hiz headlightz pull up behind mhe, so I pulled over. I waited for him to get out and walk up to my window. All I could think waz, 'I'm not goin' back again. Ain't nothin' takin' mhe tonight!' I waz scared. I didn't know what to do. I hit the gaz and took off. I hung a right onto Highland Ave. and drove near MiMom'z. Except I took a left instead of makin' a right to get to her place. I lost the cop, so I juz parked the car and sat in the woodz. I juz sat there and watched the parked car. There waz juz so much snow, but I juz sat there lookin' at the car. I thought about hoppin' back in and drivin' off. Then I saw the cop. He juz parked hiz car and waited. . . . Mom, Mom, I gotta go. He saw mhe Mom! I gotta go! I gotta go!"

Click.

"Oh my God! Oh my God! Lord, *please* protect my son!"

I called him back. It went to voicemail. I hung up.

A minute passed.

Cell phone rang; caller ID: Justin.

Deep, heavy, rapid breaths; strong, forceful, quick footsteps through the snow; tree branches snapping while being pushed out of the way.

Horrified . . ."Mom, I don't know when I'm eva gonna see you again! Mom, Mom, I love you!"

Click.

"Jesus, Jesus, JESUS! What is going *on*?!"

Immediately, I called him back . . . voicemail.

"Why do you keep calling him back?" Kelvin asked. "He keeps hanging up on you. He obviously doesn't want to talk. Just hang up the phone!"

"What? Are you crazy?! HE'S MY SON! HE NEEDS ME! I'm going to call him back until he stops calling me!"

*A minute passes . . .*Cell phone rings; caller ID: Justin.

Labored breathing. Still running.

"Justin, what are you doing? Where are you going?"

"I'm runnin' through the woodz. Mom, I can't let them catch mhe. I'm goin' to jail foreva. Man, I can't do thiz! Mom, I love you. I don't know when I'm gonna see you again. Oh my God, *Mom*! They see mhe! They see mhe! They're shinin' their flashlightz on mhe! Oh my God, they see mhe!"

Pleading . . ."Justin, stop running! Stop running through the woods! Just stop! Let them catch you! JUSTIN, PLEASE! PLEASE, LET THEM CATCH YOU!"

In desperation . . ."I can't, Mom. I can't. I can't go to jail, Mom, I can't. I gotta go, Mom. I gotta go."

Click.

"Oh, sweet Jesus, please take control of this situation. Please don't let my son take his life. Please don't let him get shot. Oh God! Please God! PLEASE . . ."

I lay in bed, weeping and wailing. My brain was saturated with emotion. My thoughts were senseless. They were racing around my mind like cars at the Indy 500. Whirls and swirls of colors and lights flashed by like lightning, leaving behind a wind tunnel. I was in the eye of a tornado, being tossed around as if I were a piece of debris. My eyes closed tightly; brow furrowed; teeth clenched; jaws tightened; pounding heart; breathing labored; stomach nauseous and knotted; lying on my side in the fetal position. I was sweating profusely. I felt helpless. I felt hopeless. I felt bound. I was losing my son.

Exhausted, I prayed, "Lord, let the police catch him. It's February. It's freezing. He's running through the woods in the snow. Let them catch him and take him where he'll be safe and warm. In Jesus's name, Amen."

My thoughts shift to my husband.

My blood was boiling, and I felt the hair standing on the back of my neck. My son had been running through the woods, and my husband asked me, "Why do you keep calling him back?" As much as I've tried, I knew at that moment I could not turn my son over to this man Lord, help my disobedience.

Four a.m., house phone rings . . .

"This is Officer Blank from the Deptford Township Police Department. We have Justin in custody. As soon as he's processed here, he'll be taken to Woodbury, where he'll be charged and processed. When they're finished with him, you'll be contacted to pick him up."

Confused . . . "Pick him up?" I confirmed.

"Yes, they'll call when he's ready."

For the next forty-five minutes, I lay, trying desperately to slow my racing mind. My head was pounding. My surroundings were spinning. My heart was throbbing. But my Justin was safe. He was not running. He was alive. He was warm. He was scared. He was crying. He was disappointed. He needed me. . . . He needed me. . . . He needed me. *Lord, I need You. . . . I need You. . . . I need You.*

Phone rang a final time. It was 5:05 a.m.

"Mrs. Hugh? This is Officer Boon from the Woodbury Police Department. We're finished processing Justin. He's being released to you. Do you know how to get here?"

Still dazed and confused. "No, I don't." He proceeded to give me directions. Realizing I did know how to get there, I was comforted. "Thank you, I should be there in twenty to thirty minutes."

Determinedly, I said, "Kelvin, I'm going to get Justin."

"You ought to just leave him where he is," he muttered.

I strengthened my inner core and sternly proclaimed, "They are releasing my son. I am going to get him."

He rose from the bed and called out of work. With few words spoken, we dressed, woke Joshua, and got in the car. As Kelvin drove, I couldn't help but ponder how it was possible Justin was being released? Why was he not being detained? I'd listened to my brother enough times to know, Justin should not be coming home. *Please, God. Don't let this be a mistake. Don't let me arrive and be told my child cannot be released. My heart is heavy and nearly shattered. I know You treasure it. Do not let this be a mistake. I prayed for him to hit rock bottom. Let this be the beginning of his fall, the beginning of the end. This is it, God. He is going to jail. This is it.*

Twenty-five minutes later we arrived at the station. It was cold, and damp with puddles of salt-melted snow scattered on the asphalt parking lot. Kelvin led the way as I safely guided a nearly sleepwalking Joshua. We entered the precinct, signed paperwork, sat down, and awaited Justin. To add insult to injury, my car had been impounded and I could not retrieve it until after nine a.m. Eventually, my son was released. Justin walked in shamefacedly into my arms, and we embraced; the weight of this experience fell off his shoulders while the weight of the future rested heavily in his eyes.

It was five forty-five a.m., and the conversation during the car ride was appropriately muted. We arrived home, and everyone retired to their beds. My mind was in a whirlwind. I couldn't sleep. I rested for an hour and determined I needed to go to work, at least for the morning. If I remained at home, I'd ponder and worry and cry, and be of no good to my already disconcerted husband, needy three-year-old, and exhausted teenager.

After a long hot shower and quiet time in prayer, I headed to work, taking Kelvin's vehicle. Although feeling better, I was too nauseous to eat breakfast. I arrived at the office shortly after opening but an hour before my first scheduled patient. I summoned my office manager into the conference room and closed the door. All the strength I had previously mustered up gradually left my body as I recounted the night's events through tear-filled eyes. True to her character, she comforted, extended empathy, then urged me to go home. After further conversation, she understood my *need* to work, at least until lunchtime, when I could retrieve my car. Determined to provide good pediatric care with a smile, I squared my shoulders and greeted my patients behind a mask of idealism.

Much to Justin's dismay, after only six hours of sleep, he was awakened to accompany the family to reclaim the vehicle for which he was responsible for impounding. This was not the time for recuperating sleep but for manifesting responsibility. This was the time for deliberately discussing the changing dynamics of the Hugh household; for recognizing, once again, that there was a consequence for every action, whether good, bad, or indifferent. We would then wait for that inevitable piece of mail, the letter that would summon us to court—and to the consequence of Justin's actions.

Over the next month, I watched my son operate from hopeful expectation in the face of an assured loss of freedom. On March 4, the inevitable piece of mail arrived: "You are to appear for a preliminary hearing on Thursday, March 17." That was it. Thirteen days. When that day came, the judge ordered one month for referrals and evaluations to be completed. The state's disposition included the following recommendations: one-year loss of license, thirty-month probation with referral to a juvenile residential community home, or eighteen month's incarceration with a program on a committed status. The disposition date was scheduled for Monday, April 18.

Despondent. Discontent. Dejected. How do you function when your fate has been given a date with a mournful destiny; when your destination of hopeful expectancy has been turned one hundred eighty degrees? You disengage and vacate the structure that contains your soul and spirit. You leave behind a carcass of who you used to be. How do I nurture such a shell? How do I discover my purpose for such a time as this? How does my heart shift to fertilizing my disoriented son while seeking solace in its brokenness? God must prepare him for his destiny, and me for mine.

"He who dwells in the secret place of the Most High shall abide under the shadow of the Almighty. I will say of the Lord, 'He is my refuge and my fortress: My God, in Him will I trust.' Because he has set his love upon Me, therefore I will deliver him; I will set him on high, because he has known My name. He shall call upon Me, and I will answer him; I will be with him in trouble; I will deliver him and honor him. With long life I will satisfy him and show him My salvation" (Psalms 91: 1–2; 14–16 NKJV).

I possessed a stark ambivalence between knowing my son would be in a safe, protected environment where all his physical needs would be met, and knowing his emotional and spiritual needs would be challenged daily. Justin's desires vacillated between the restrained freedom of a residential facility and prolonged probation, and eighteen months incarceration and presumably assured freedom after that. On Friday, April 15, we realized all the referrals and evaluations for placement into a residential facility had been negated. His fate had materialized. He would inevitably face incarceration. The question then was: For how long did *we* have to serve?

The story of Mary of Bethany is one centered on worship.

Luke 10:38–42 relays an interaction between two sisters, Mary, and Martha, whose brother, Lazarus, had died four days prior. Jesus and His disciples entered a village called Bethany. Martha welcomed them into her home. Mary seated herself at Jesus's feet and continually listened as He taught. Martha was very busy and distracted with all her serving responsibilities. She approached Jesus and began to complain: "Are you not concerned that my sister has left me to do all the serving alone? Tell her to help me and do her part."

He replied, "Martha, Martha, you are worried and bothered and anxious about so many things, but only one thing is necessary, for Mary has chosen the good part (that which is to her advantage), which will not be taken away from her." She had taken the posture of a disciple. She had chosen to worship!

"Worship is where we find our true identities. When we kneel to worship—humbling ourselves before God and acknowledging His rule over our lives—we discover why we were created." (Grady 2012, 166).

I found myself in a faith crisis when my son was running through the woods. He was in a state of brokenness and despair. Just as Mary was not distracted by her sister's pleading, I was not distracted by my husband's opposition. I held firmly to my faith and worshipped God through prayer. I had spent enough hours with my heart surrendered, mind engaged, and will yielded, to know that even when I could not see God's hand, I knew how to trust His plan. I knew how to press into His presence. In that moment, I knew my son needed to be covered. It was not about what my husband thought. It was not even about what I thought. It was about what Justin needed. In that moment I chose reckless abandonment and laid it all on the line for the saving of his mind.

QUESTIONS TO CONSIDER

1. How often has your past made you run?
2. From what fears are you now running?
3. What thing has brought you face-to-face with your ultimate fear?
4. What steps can you take to increase your devotion to God?

WORDS OF ENCOURAGEMENT

No matter how far, no matter the terrain, you can never outrun God's desire and ability to save you.

SONG FOR YOUR SEASON

"I Surrender All"—CeCe Winans

ACT OF KINDNESS

Make plans today to conquer your greatest fear.

CHAPTER FIVE

It Takes Courage

The strain and discord that Justin's behaviors have on my marriage were evidenced by Kelvin's rising and leaving for work at his usual five a.m. He elected not to accompany me to court, telling me, "You have your brother for support." I had no appetite for breakfast, and watching my son drag himself out of bed and knowing he'd be resting his head in a jail cell by night's end was nearly more than my heart could bear. We stoically embraced as he emerged from his bedroom. Our eyes shifted, avoiding sustained contact, lest either would falter to tears.

I wake up with thoughtz of suicide but I can't bring myself to actually try any of them. I juz wanna run away. Nowhere in particular. Juz run. All the thoughtz I eva had about prison are pacin' through my head. I can't help but think of my girlfriend. I love her so much. Iz she gonna wait for mhe like she said she will? Iz she gonna cheat on mhe? Somethin' makez it hard to find trust. I'm not even concerned for my safety. I'm scared. I juz can't figure it out. How can I run and make thiz all go away? Thiz iz the day I figured out what true fear iz.

Dropping Joshua off at day care created a difficult divide. I allowed my sons enough time to say good-bye. The twenty-minute ride to the courthouse was filled with tender thoughts, encouraging and affirming words, anxiety regarding the immediate and long-term unknowns, and anticipation for the beginning of the end.

Leavin' the houz, walkin' to the car, and gettin' in really, really suckz. It iz utterly agonizin' and depressin'. I know itz my fault. I have no one to blame but myself. Thiz iz my inevitable fate. And yet, I have no choice. I must do thiz. Itz like I am havin' an out of body experience. Like I'm bein' dragged along. I am helpless. I have lost control ova my own destiny.

Once in the courthouse, outside the courtroom, we met with my younger brother, Brian, and reviewed the state's disposition: eighteen months incarceration with no objection to programs on a committed status. All efforts to abort the inevitable have failed.

I have lost all hope for a different outcome. I continued textin' my girlfriend. I need assurance that she iz gonna hold

mhe down through all of thiz. All I really care about iz thiz
relationship. I am obsessed with it. Right now, I can't think
of anyone else.

No longer are we able to hold back the tears. The final weight of this journey was more than either of us could bear. Amid it all, Justin's mind found a way to rebel against his heart. He paced back and forth, saying, "No, I'm not goin'. I'm not built for thiz. I'm not goin'. Maybe they can put mhe on house arrest for a year, or even two. But I can't go to jail. I can't do thiz" While I stood comforting him through my tears, Brian facilitated reason and reassurance as Justin's attorney, and stern resolution as his uncle. After a reasonable amount of time, Justin gathered and calmed himself.

I just stood there, staring at my son. Staring at his face, every facet of it. Trying to find *him* in his eyes. Rather, discovering lost hope, I scanned his body from top to bottom.

"Take off your hat, take out your earrings, take off your watch, take off your belt, and empty your pockets."

"No, Mom . . . No . . . I can't do thiz."

"Justin, you have to. They are gonna make you take it off when they take you to the back. Just give it to me.

Give it to me now. Wouldn't you rather I have possession of them than the state?" He released them to me as we proceeded into the courtroom.

"All rise, the Honorable Judge . . .presiding. You may be seated."

April 18, 2011

Eighteen months incarceration with no objection to programs on a committed status. At
the New Jersey Training School for Boys in Jamesburg.

"Do you wish to tell me anything, son?" the judge asked.

"No," Justin replied.

"So now comes the point where I get to tell you something, okay? I looked at the files. I read the reports of everything that's come back to me. Listen, I understand it's traumatic to you. Get him some tissues. I'm not an expert. I'm not a psychologist. I don't know what's going on. Based on everyone that you've spoken to, there appears to be a point in time when your mother decided to move on with her life and get married. That is when things started to become problematic for you in the household. A lot of the issues that you have stem from your mother's relationship with her husband, and your relationship with your stepfather. And, son, I don't know why that is. I can't answer that question. I've looked in the file. I've looked to see if you really told anybody why your mother's marriage is an issue. It appears to me that your natural dad is still in the picture. He's a father to you. Someone I know your stepfather never sought to replace, but your father has been married a couple of times, and that didn't cause you any issues.

"So I'm not sure, and this is what I want you to focus on. I'm not sure if it really is about your stepfather. Maybe it is. But maybe it's about something else. Maybe the issue about you saying your stepfather is the problem is something convenient because you don't want to tell everybody else what the real problem is. Because, if your stepfather situation is the real problem, okay, then you're gonna need to work on that and focus on yourself. Unless there's something really out of the way that's not in these records, then it's an issue you have to work on. Because, your mother shouldn't be here, and I hope she's not feeling guilty because she decided to move on with her life. And your stepfather shouldn't feel he's the cause of your problems, because he didn't jump in a car and run away from the police. You understand what I'm saying? Can you answer me?"

"Yes."

"So my concern is, you seem like an intelligent man. And if that's what it is, the work needs to be done on your end. But if that's not what it is, if it's something else that's going on, then this is an opportunity for you to be clear about it. For you to really tell somebody about it. Get some help for it. Because if the stepfather is the problem, then let's deal with that. But if it's not, if it's something else, and that just became a convenient crutch for you to use as an excuse, it doesn't make any sense to me. It really doesn't make a whole lot of sense the way I see it. I think it's something else. I think something else is going on in your life. Something else is going on inside you, and you're not getting help for it, and you're not able to deal with it. And that's why we're where we are. That's what I think. I can't be sure because only you can answer that question. Only you can answer that question.

"Now, in this circumstance, I'm gonna want to know what's going on. I'm gonna want to see if you avail yourself to some help. And I'm gonna want to see, basically, how you're doing. I'm gonna want a report done after six months. I'm gonna want to see where you are. If there have been some revelations, if your behavior is appropriate, if you're making strides, If you're getting past these issues, or if we've come up with what the real issues are, and you've sought some help for it, and you're on your way, I'll look at this. I'll take a look at you again. I'll see where we are. You understand?"

"Yes."

"So it's not really out of your control. It is, now? It is for a short period of time. I mean, six months is a long time for any young man. But it should start now. Do you understand, Justin?"

"Yes."

"You have any questions for me?"

"No."

"All right. Justin, are you afraid?"

"Yes."

"All right. Are you angry?"

"Yes."

"All right. These are things you're going to have to deal with. You understand?"

"Yes."

"Do you have any other questions for me?"

"No."

The appeals process was discussed.

[Brian] began by saying, "Judge, I've been doing criminal defense work since 2003. I have to say, I've been involved in difficult cases with difficult outcomes. But this is the saddest day I have ever had to come to court. You know, Justin knows I have been talking to him for a long time. For two and a half years, to get him more opportunities, to get him the help that he needed, and quite frankly, he's been bestowed a great many opportunities and benefits by the state, and the resources that are available. It's just sad that though he hasn't been completely without progress, there aren't more signs of rehabilitation. And, I'm so sorry to see how he's wasted all these opportunities that have been bestowed, especially the one that was given to you in December. When he came home and when he was looking at a residential program, he got accepted into one at that time. He messed it up in less than two months. So I have been talking to him a lot about this."

Brian directed his attention to Justin: "Justin, now, you created this difficult path for yourself. You chose the difficult fork in the road. But you got to walk the walk, and you're strong enough to survive it despite your fear, despite your anger. You only have yourself to be angry with. But at the same time, you can use this as a new beginning to your life and not an end to your life. That could happen if you make the wrong choices when you get down here. And the judge just spoke to you about wanting to review your case after six months. And we talked in the hallway about how you may leave here and just say I don't care. This is the time. If you've never cared about yourself before, Justin, you better start caring right now 'cause this can mark the beginning of your life anew. You'll have no criminal record as an adult. You can still make something out of your life, or you can end your life right now. The choice is gonna be up to you, and you got to start making better choices."

The judge chimed in. "I completely agree. Look, it's a sad day for me, but emotions don't impact my decisions. And we talked about it when Mom and Dad were here before. We see the family that's here and the opportunities. You know, you talked about rehabilitation before. Justin, I don't think it's about rehabilitation with you. Something's wounded in you that has to be healed. I don't think it's about you being a criminal element, okay. I don't see you like that. I see that there's something wrong, but you're just not giving anybody the opportunity to intervene. You're not surrendering yourself to say, 'You know what—everybody that's been telling me all this stuff, and they're right. And I want to live in society, and I want to live a happy life, and I don't want to be angry. I don't want to be afraid. I want to move forward and be happy.'

"If you want happiness, you're going to have to surrender in terms of taking your guard down and letting somebody in and letting someone really know what is going on because I haven't seen that. I have not seen that. I read the reports, and there are unanswered questions. And it's not just about, you know. Does Justin have psychiatric issues? Does Justin have psychological issues? Something's going on, son, and until you tell us, we're limited in what we can do to help you. But, as soon as you tell us, this system is here to do everything it can to help you. It's the nature of the system. And not only that, but unlike most people sitting in that chair, you've got family and you've got your own resources where your family can help you. So I wish you the best of luck. And, I will . . . Justin, I *will* . . . . You think I'm gonna forget this case? You know I know you. You understand that?"

"Yes."

"And I will be here after that six-month time. And I know your mother is going to want me to look at this case, and your father and your stepfather are gonna want me to look at this case, and Mr. Hill is gonna want me to look at this case. And when this case comes back for review, I will look at it. And we'll see where you are. You understand what that means?"

"Yes."

"Do you think you can take advantage of that opportunity?"

"Yes."

"All right, Justin, I wish you the best. I hope I get good news because I don't need you in there. All right? Officer, let him say goodbye to his mom."

Everything that judge said went in one ear and out the other. How he talkin' to mhe like he know mhe? I feel disrespected. All I wanna do iz murder everyone in the room and run away. I know it seemz stupid and impossible, but that'z all I got right now. Man, I'm scared! I'm scared of Jamesburg! I'm in a desperate situation and there iz no way out. Man, I'm about to go crazy right now. I ain't tryin' to hear what you sayin' right now. I take offense to all thiz. You ain't tryin' to help mhe! You're takin' mhe away from my home! I feel numb. Very, very numb. I can't even believe thiz iz happenin'. I don't even want to go through the motionz. Man, I'm pissed! Whatever it iz, it iz.

As I sat listening to this judge commit my son to eighteen months incarceration, I was bewildered. I had a seemingly insurmountable weight of grief as my head ached, my eyes were wide-open, my mouth was dry, my breathing was deeply labored, my chest felt like it was going to cave in, and I was sweating profusely. Yet, I am altogether baffled by what I just heard. Did I just hear this judge say he wants to see Justin back in six months? Like, is there actually a possibility of him being released after six months, not eighteen?! Did this judge just encourage my son? Did I hear him say he did not see my son as a criminal element? That there was something troubling him deep down on the inside that he was not surrendering to? That he needed to put his guard down and let someone in for healing to begin? You mean, you saw value in my son? You saw my son's life as worthy? You said, "I don't need you in there." My God. My God!

I walked over to look Justin in the eyes one last time as our eyes flooded with tears. We embraced briefly but tightly and exchanged "I love you" before the bailiff took him away.

The bailiff put the cuffz on my wrists, and I put the "tough man" on my face. I am led to the back where I am shackled and sat on a long bench beside other newly convicted juvenilez waitin' to get shipped to a correctional facility. Itz cold. The lightz are bright. The room is filled with the voicez of police officers talkin' all loud. Making jokz about being hungry and us not goin' home with our familiz.

Back in the same hallway where we gathered before

entering the courtroom, Brian and I sat speaking with a representative from the Juvenile Justice Commission. Her voice was soft and reassuring as she detailed where Justin was going, what the process was like, and what was to be expected. It was as if I was suspended in time. Her words floated whimsically around my head as my heart searched for meaning in the moment. I felt numb; very, very numb.

I thanked, embraced, and said goodbye to my brother. Recognizing the distraught and anguished look on my face, he asked with great concern, "Are you okay? Do you want me to go with you? Are you sure you're okay to drive home? Why don't we stop by MumMum's first?"

Meekly, I said, "Yes. Yes, I'm okay. I don't want to stop by MumMum's. I would rather be alone. I need to be alone. Will you please call Mommie and Daddy and let them know what happened? I just cannot make those calls right now."

"Of course, of course. Call me when you get home."

"Okay."

Driving with my hands firmly set at ten and two, and my eyes fixed on the road, my heart broke into a thousand little pieces. Hyperventilating and crying aloud, I searched to find meaning in that moment, in that season.

Lord, he's my son, but he belongs to You. I've done as much as I could. I've protected him from as much as I could. I've shielded him from so much. I've modeled honesty, integrity, and love. I warned him, if you continue doing what you're doing, you will find yourself living outside of this home. This loving, nurturing, safe environment will no longer be an oasis for you. You will not appreciate what we've provided for you until it's gone. It's gone. It's gone. It's gone!

Lord, it's all out of my hands. My child, my first born, my son, is out of my safety. He's out of my arms of protection. He's away from my love. He's out of my home. Lord, cover him. Keep him. Protect him from all manner of hurt, harm, and danger. He belongs to You. This cannot be the end. This cannot be his story. This cannot be what You have purposed for his life. You did not bring me to this place for it to be the end. This is not how my story will end. You've called me unto Yourself. You've walked with me all these years, through all my trials. There is no way this is the end.

So Lord, I surrender it all to You. Thank You for allowing me stewardship over him. The only way he's going to make it out of this place is through You. The only way I am going to stand in this place is through You. Lord, I prayed for him to hit rock bottom, and he has. You are a prayer-answering God. He's at the lowest place he's ever been, and as

You are my witness, and with Your strength, I will go within one inch of his lowest place. I will go as far down as I need to go, so that when he turns his head to look up, the first face he will always see is mine. I will not allow another in the place where I belong. He will not rely on the strength, love, and support of another. I am his mother. You blessed and entrusted me with his life. I will not let him down.

Speak to his heart right now! Settle his troubled mind, right now! Your Word says You have prepared a table before me in the presence of my enemies. Lord, set the table before Justin right now. Like Job, let the enemy try as he may to destroy him, but my God, don't let him touch his life, and don't let him touch his mind. Do what You have to do to get what You have to get. All the while, I will continue to serve You. I will continue to worship You. I will continue to bless Your name, for You are good and Your mercy and truth endure to all generations.

Let this season be a testimony of Your goodness and love. Of Your grace and mercy. Of Your strength and power. My God, I give my son to You without reservation or condition. It is the most difficult moment I've had to face as a mother, but even more, I believe, if You brought me to this, it is once again You that will bring me through it. Settle now my heart and my mind. Equip me for this battle. Strengthen me for this journey. Help me to be a good mother to Joshua, and an even better wife to Kelvin. In Jesus's name, amen.

I can't even believe I'm here. Thiz iz so depressin' knowin' I'm not goin' home. Four white concrete wallz with two, small windowz, a high ceiling, and a bed. A small air vent on either side separatez mhe from two other roomz. Here I sit, sad and scared, wearing a blue jumper and sneakerz.

At some point I fell asleep. I don't even know how I fell asleep. I don't even remember fallin' asleep. I juz' woke up feelin' like I have no heart. I'm goin' to prison. I don't know how to fight. I don't know how I'm gonna survive.

DEVOTIONAL ANECDOTE:

A LESSON FROM JOCHEBED

†

The story of Jochebed is one of remarkable courage.
Exodus 1:15–22; 2:1–10

The King of Egypt said to the Hebrew midwives, whose names were Shiphrah and Puah, "When you are helping the Hebrew women during childbirth on the delivery stool, if you see that the baby is a boy, kill him; but if it is a girl, let her live." The midwives, however, feared God and did not do what the King of Egypt had told them to do. They let the boys live.

The King of Egypt summoned the midwives and asked them, "Why have you done this? Why have you let the boys live?" The midwives answered Pharaoh, "Hebrew women are not like Egyptian women; they are vigorous and give birth before midwives arrive."

So God was kind to the midwives, and the people increased and became even more numerous. And because the midwives feared God, he gave them families of their own.

Then Pharaoh gave this order to all his people: "Every Hebrew boy that is born must be thrown into the Nile, but let every girl live."

Now, a man of the tribe of Levi married a Levite woman, and she became pregnant and gave birth to a son. When she saw that he was a fine child, she hid him for three months. But when she could hide him no longer, she got a papyrus basket for him and coated it with tar and pitch. Then she placed the child in it and put it among the reeds along the bank of the Nile.

His sister stood at a distance to see what would happen to him.

Then Pharaoh's daughter went down to the Nile to bathe, and her attendants were walking along the riverbank. She saw the basket among the reeds and sent her female slaves to get it. She opened it and saw the baby. He was crying, and she felt sorry for him. "This is one of the Hebrews' babies," she said.

Then his sister asked Pharaoh's daughter, "Shall I go and get one of the Hebrew women to nurse the baby for you?"

"Yes, go," she answered. So the girl went and got the

baby's mother. Pharaoh's daughter said to her, "Take this baby and nurse him for me, and I will pay you." So the woman took the baby and nursed him.

When the child grew older, she took him to Pharaoh's daughter, and he became her son. She named him Moses, saying, "I drew him out of the water."

Jochebed was a woman of remarkable courage. Her actions were an ironic reversal of Abraham's in Genesis, Chapter 22. Abraham obeyed God's order to kill his son Isaac, yet Isaac's life was spared. Jochebed disobeyed Pharaoh's order to kill Moses, and Moses's life was spared. God honored Abraham's obedience while at the same time honoring Jochebed's defiance. How could this be so? By faith, she obeyed God and defied the law of the land as it was in disobedience with God's Word.

Everyone is afraid of someone or something. Everyone will, at some point in their lives, be motivated by fear. Be motivated by fearing God; by having a sense of respect, submission, and awe. Do what you know is right in the face of pain and grief. Chose to confront agony, pain, uncertainty, or intimidation without wavering. Oppose the areas of danger and difficulty without fear. I did.

Like Jochebed, I came to understand the paradox of

humility: he who is humbled will be exalted. And the realization that to hold him, we had to let him go. We let go of a child who belonged to God more than he ever belonged to us.

QUESTIONS TO CONSIDER

1. What is the most courageous thing you have ever done?
2. What does fear look like for you?
3. What do you need to let go of to grab hold of it again?
4. What loss do you need to mourn to treasure happiness?

WORDS OF ENCOURAGEMENT

"It is the fire of suffering that brings forth the gold of godliness."—Jeanne Marie Bouvier de la Motte Guyon

SONG FOR YOUR SEASON

"He's Not on His Knees Yet"—CeCe Winans

ACT OF KINDESS

Encourage someone to do something brave.

CHAPTER SIX
†
Letters from the Heart

May 8, 2011

To my Wonderful Mother,

I juz' wanna let you know how much I love you. I want you to know how happy I am to have you as a mother. I know how much you sacrifice for mhe and I want you to know one day, I'm gonna pay you back for all the stress, tearz, and hourz of lost sleep you've given over mhe. There'z no other person in my life that I would lay my life down for. My love for you is beyond unconditional. Mom, I would do anything for you. When it comez down to love, I really can't explain how much of it I have for you. You've been such a good mother and friend to mhe my entire life. You been there for mhe since the day I was born. You've been there at my little league gamez and you been there when I needed someone to talk to. You've housed mhe, clothed mhe, and gave mhe so much that I know I don't deserve. But, what iz really most important to mhe iz that you never gave up on mhe, even after I started getting locked up. Even the second time I'm goin' away, ya still here for mhe. And I am so thankful for that. Mom, I love you to death and I want you to know that I won't be gone forever. I'll be home before the year iz over. So juz' keep ya head up. I miss & love you so much. Happy Mother'z Day!—Justin

May 17, 2011

Mom,

I got to Jamesburg today and I hate this place. I swear to God, I'm never gettin' locked up again. But anyway, I talk to parole and classification in two weekz and they will tell mhe if I can go to a Program. Please pray that I do. I don't wanna stay here until August. But anyway, I wanna let you know I love you and I miss you. Please write mhe back before I leave JRU in two weekz. Tell Kelvin I sed wassup. I'll call when I can. I love you—Justin

Sunday, May 22, 2011

Hi Justin,

Just to give you a timeline, you wrote me the letter on Wednesday and I got it on Friday.

I'm sorry to hear you hate that place, but I'm glad to hear you say you're never getting locked up again. I truly hope you mean it. I knew that place was not for you and I did everything in my power to keep you from experiencing it for yourself. Now that you are there, and do not have the power to change that fact, for the next six months (well five now), you need to focus on what you do have the power to change. You are in control of not adding additional days to your time. You control the quality of the time you're obligated to spend there. You need to purpose in your mind that you are through with relinquishing that much power to anyone or anything else in your life. That which controls has all the power. Take control now! It's not too late.

If you have not already, try to see your days in parts rather than the whole. Maybe you have been there long enough to see how to break them down. That will make the time seem more manageable. Once again, you still have control over how you experience your time there.

Now, I will pray for you as I always do and that you will choose to walk in the way God has planned and purposed for your life; even this most difficult walk. Until you decide to submit to His will and way, it doesn't matter what my prayer is. God knows the outcome in the next two weeks. As your mother, I want what's best for you. If your being placed in a program after two weeks is best, then so be it. If what's best for you, to really embed in your mind that this really is not the lifestyle you want to live, is for you to spend two months in "whatever" it is they term it to be, then so be it. I don't want the easy way out for you. I want you to walk the path that is going to lead to permanent change for your life. I want you to have an awesome testimony for other teenagers and pre-teens when you are done with this place. Prayerfully, the two weeks you must do in JRU will be enough. If the officers and Classification Board say otherwise, then you need to be prepared to handle that reality. So, use these two weeks to prepare yourself mentally and emotionally for the worst possible outcome. Pray that God will prepare you for what He has planned for you. Don't always pray for tough situations to go away. You build strength and endurance from going through difficult times, not going around them. Pray for God's "uncommon favor." I want you to learn that term. Understand what it means and the implications for praying for that outcome. Uncommon means unusual. The unexpected. Underserved. Favor is preference. You want God to be merciful and grant you what you do not deserve; to give you undeserved, unusual preference the entire time you are there. But, that does not mean getting the easy way out. It means coming out through the pathway that will lead to the greatest chance for a changed life when you come home. You want your life to be 180 degrees different than it was on May 16, 2011. Think about that and begin to make it happen.

I love you and I know you can make it through this. I too must endure and be strengthened through all this. My faith is strong, and I know that as difficult as it is for me, as a mother, it's more difficult for you, as you are the one away from home. Cry all the tears that are necessary for you to cry. Tears are not for the weak; they are for the humble. God will raise your head when you feel you can't. Pride goeth before the fall. Don't be too proud, lest you fall. Pray daily and often. When you are weak, that's when God is made strong in you.

Take care my son. Feel the strength of my love in the letters I write. Come home to your family a changed young man. I will write you back with each letter you send. Try not to overlap them.

Praying for you and missing you.

Love, Mommie

Thursday, May 26, 2011

Mom,

First lemme say, when I got your letter, I broke down crying. You made me feel so guilty and I know that wasn't your intention. Itz juz' that I love you so much and Itz hurtin' mhe to know what I'm putting you threw. Mom, I'm so sorry for everything wrong I've ever done to you or sed to you. You are such a wonderful woman and you don't deserve to have a son that actz the way I do. You've always been there for mhe no matter what it waz and I thank you for that. I love you so much Mom.

IDK if thiz iz a question that you have, but just in case it iz, I haven't been fightin' and I'm not going to. I know I need to go home ASAP so I'm doing everything in my power to make sure that happenz . . . Now, when I see Classification, I will see if I can do a community program. Some people say that they only give you pointz by the chargez you are locked up for. Now and if that'z the case, I should be eligible for a community program from the rip. I'm makin' a promise to you now, if I get a program, I'm not gonna run. I don't want to run. My time iz short and I'm juz' gonna eat it up and get home. So, if Campus iz an option, please don't object to it. I know you sed God will put mhe where I need to be, so if that opportunity comez up, please juz' go with it. You can trust mhe. Whether you believe it or not, ever since I caught my charge, I've done a lot of growing up.

Juz' in case I do go on groundz instead of a program, could you send mhe some money? They don't feed uz a lot and you can buy canteen here. Also, you can get ya haircut and uze tha phone. But tha phone iz like a dollar a minute so I'm not makin' callz unless I get one from my social worker. Tha money haz to be sent through the mail, by certified check or a money order. They sed you can get it at any post office. Oh and plus, in JRU, they put stampz on tha letterz for you. But on groundz, I have to purchase stampz. So, if you could, could you send mhe some? Thankz.

So, thatz all I have to say for now until you write mhe agen. Oh wait, juz' to let you know tha kidz here are chill. That whole North Jerzey kidz beefin' wit South Jerzey thing ain't true. Everybody juz' tryin' to get they time over wit. An' I found out that they got a full studio on groundz too, wit guitarz and all that. So if I gotta go there, you know I'm tryin' spend az much time az possible in there. So there'z some positive to this.

So juz' keep ya head up Mom. I'll be home before you know it. Day 38. 142 to go. I love you sooo much. Tell Kelvin and Joshua I sed wassup. Byeee—Justin

Monday, June 13, 2011

Hey Justin,

I didn't write you last week because I had spoken to you on the phone for quite a while. You should have gotten my note and a money order by now. Also, Aunt Jamila and grand mom have also written and sent you money. Hopefully, you'll have enough in your account to hold you for a while.

Kelvin said, be careful with your purchases. Now that you are in common quarters with so many other youths, I think you told me 40, there tends to be the formation of cliques. Guys begin to hang out and build ties with one another. They also tend to steal from each other. Not everyone can afford to have people send them money. Purchase what you need on an as-needed basis. Don't try to stockpile your stuff so people see what you have. Don't talk to people about how much money you have been sent. You don't need people jealous of you and seeking to intimidate you over what your family is able to afford.

Keep yourself focused, especially with school. Don't be duped. I know you said that you're pretty much sitting around "chillin'," but, you have to earn credits and gain knowledge to advance once you leave that place. So, it is not to your advantage to sit around and chill. Let the people know you're the type of guy who takes the initiative and ask questions. Find something to do. Find other ways to increase your knowledge. Remember, they should be grooming you to enroll in a program at Camden County College to obtain your high school diploma and college credit simultaneously. You want to be in a position to compete at a level greater than where you are now. If that means you go the extra mile when no one else does, that's what you do.

Are you able to participate in any other programs where you are, or do you have to wait until your 90 days are up? I received a copy of your time goal determination report. It seems as though you've been favored once again. The judge sentenced you to 18 months, but the parole board gave you a time goal of 12 months.

Also, they made suggestions for mental health, substance abuse, alcohol, and anger management programs. Have you begun any of those? I hope you don't have to wait 90 days to begin. You need ample time to participate and complete those programs satisfactorily. You don't want to come out and not have the tools you need to be successful and not slip back into old thought processes.

Pop-Pop and G-Ma are coming to New Jersey June 12 through 22. I'm giving Kelvin a surprise retirement party on

June 18 from 7 p.m–10 p.m. Rev. Walker, Min. Adrienne,
and Min. Franklin will be there. So far, it's still a surprise.
I've been busy the last week and for sure will be this week
with the final touches. I'll keep you posted or should I say,
I'll let you know how it all goes.

Power of God is this week at church. Women of Judah
danced for the Sunday night kick-off. We have to dance Fri-
day for the closing. T.D. Jakes will be preaching that night.
It's going to be crazy at the Plaza. I think the only other
night I'll go is Thursday. Noel Jones will be there that night.
I won't be there tonight because Joshua has his three-year-old
promotional exercise at school. I still remember when you
were three years old at Camden Day Nursery. I took pictures
of Joshua, but they were dark, and his tie was crooked in all
four poses. We didn't order any. We'll dress him up and take
him to the mall and get pictures done, or maybe Walmart.
That's less expensive.

I've been taking sermon notes with you in mind. Since
they're on my iPod, I can email them to myself and print
them out. I've decided to do this for you, so you have some
encouraging material to read. Get your hands on a Bible
so you can read the scriptures pertaining to the sermons. I
have included two in this mailing. Next time, I'll send one
at a time. Let me know what you think, after you've had a

chance to study them. Of course, I pray for you daily. I know you are going to come out of this a stronger young man.

Continue to be encouraged. It is 7:45 a.m. and I have to get ready for work. Love you honey and bunches. Have a blessed week. Write back when you can. By the way, I'm keeping my chin up; you do the same—Mommie

*M*O*T*H*E*R*

You pray cuz ya problems don't attract God'z attention
*   Dat'z Lesson #1 of ya Devine Intervention*
*   Lesson #2 iz resign and repenting*
*   Cuz time could be short*
*   Like money off a pension*
*   Itz betta to know how to think than to do what you*
think
*   A word from the wize, to life, dat word iz a link*
*   Feed a man for a day, juz' give him a fish*
*   Or feed a man for a lifetime and teach him to fish*
*   You gotta grow up and man up, no youth iz infinity*
*   Hatred needz a host and it don't live inside of mhe*
*   You fight a war, kill and die for pride and ya dignity*
*   But in the dark, you can't see who has the true victory*
*   When the right hand helpz, don't let the left know he'z*
doin' it
*   Tha good iz done in private, tha blessin' iz openly*
*   But tha world will turn around and what they say will*
oppose to mhe
*   "If I can't tell the deed, then forget tha integrity."*

Dat'z human, but to God murder and boast iz equal
A sin iz a sin, but tha devil liez to you people
He makez you believe that to life, there'z a sequel
But death on tha lake of fire are the wagez of evil.
Christianity in diz world iz barely even heard of
All they really care about iz Sex, Money, and Murder
A young girl would be taken in but tossed if they can't
convert her
But Jesus Christ would take her and neva eva dessert her
You need to think before you sin, juz' cuz you are mad
Don't turn ya head to mhe, Lissen! Tha wordz come
from our Dad
Jesus spoke, "Let tha one w/o sin do the cast"
Remember, vengeance iz tha Lordz You need to let tha
hate pass
Before you run you must learn to crawl
Then you learn to stand. Then you learn to walk
But before you walk, you must learn to crawl
And when you learn to stand, don't be scared to fall
Build tha strength in ya legz and be prepared for all
When the Devil attackz, itz like wood to a saw
One lifeline left there ain't no time to stall
God iz on the phone, will you answer the call?

That's a poem I wrote. I been doin' some song writin' and thought I'd switch it up and make somthin' different. I thought I'd send it to you, so I could get some opinionz on it. So, Lemme know what you and anyone you decide to show it to thinkz.

So, to answer ya questionz. No, I am not able to participate in any programz. I have to wait until August 1. Then I will be eligible for a community program. Juz' count on October 18. But I will pray for Godz uncommon favor. And hopefully He will bless mhe and get mhe home at the end of September. And, my max is still 10/18/12. My "tentative" release date is 3/27/12. That'z the latest they want mhe out az of right now. But, if I keep ma nose clean and go back to court on 10/18 w/all good reportz and no extra chargez, I will come home on probation. No matter what, I cannot be held in custody past 10/18/12.

I've been doin' a lot of connecting with God and he'z tellin' mhe somthin'. He haz something planned for mhe. An I think itz big. Satan knoz it too cuz he'z doin' everything possible to make mhe mess up so I can't go home ASAP. He wantz to keep mhe locked up. But I've learned how to let wordz be wordz. I'm done lettin' other people gaz mhe up. So, if ya worried about mhe fightin', stop. It will not happen.

Well mom I love you. I'm keeping ma head up. Time iz short. 120 dayz, four monthz, 16 weekz however you wanna look at it. I'll be home in no time. Stay Strong—Justin

P.S. I want you to know, I think about you every day. Itz probably harder on you than it iz on mhe. I really don't stress that much. Maybe once or twice on Fridayz and Saturdayz . . . And why stress anyway? My time is short Mom. There'z (guyz) down here w/ 3, 4, 5 yearz and I'm gonna be home in October. Maybe September. So, if ya stressin' stop. Don't worry about thingz you have no control over. Parole and the Judge are tha only people that can send mhe home. Well, God too. But, like I sed, time is short. Four monthz, well less now. Juz' keep ya head high. Situationz are only temporary. I juz' felt I had to add a lil somthin' cuz this letter seemed short. But yeah, I love you Mom. I'll be home soon. Write back ASAP.—Justin

Sunday, July 31, 2011

Hey Justin!

Joshua and I had a most fantastic visit with you today!!

On my drive there, I was really kind of queasy in my stomach. I was nervous and psyched at the same time. Although I felt bad because none of your other unit mates had visitors. I'm relieved that Joshua had a chance to see you and ask the difficult questions that he did. He really does miss you. He may not understand time in the 24-hour, 7-day-a-week sense that we do, but he realizes his brother has been gone a while now.

I was especially glad to see and have confirmed what I'd been hearing when I speak to you on the phone. You really have begun to mature in your thought process and understand actions, consequences, and responsibility. It's just the beginning so, it's not time for you to come home yet. You definitely need the time remaining to perfect, or should I say, for God to perfect in you, what He has started. He did not bring you this far to leave you. He did bring you this far to stretch, mold, redeem, and promote you. Meditate on those four things when you have your quiet time with Him.

A mother's heart is never at rest when one of her children is out of her care. What I can do is rest on my faith in God, knowing you're in His care and that is the only care that trumps mine! I used to tell you all the time, and I will continue to tell you, God has entrusted you to the care of two human beings, Naomi Hill, and Gregory Mitchell. I am wholeheartedly responsible for how I support, provide for, and raise you. Your dad has to answer for himself. I will not be slack in my stewardship over you. Mothering is an awesome responsibility and privilege; and is like unto no other. Until the day the Lord calls me home, my job will never be done. Sure, there will come a time, when you are grown and responsible and accountable to Him 100%. But, I believe, there is still a portion of mothering that will always be present; a part that will never cease to be complete as long as my lungs have breath. So, I hope you have come to know and understand why I pray the way I do. Why I ache the way I do. Why my mind races when you are in trouble, and why storms rage in my heart when you are in trouble. Not only when you are in trouble, but when you are troubled. There is a part of my spirit that will always remain attached to you. I feel things when you are unsettled that you don't know that I feel. I experience joy in my spirit when you have a spiritual breakthrough. It's just a matter of fact. That's why I say, there are people attached to your life that are gravely affected by your choices. Choose wisely for yourself and for those whom you represent. Right now, I applaud you for being on the right track.

When I arrived at Church immediately after our visit, the Spirit was making Himself known in the sanctuary. It was time to pray and hold hands. I had just whispered to Minister Mary Hodge (the one who is involved with JJC through the Prison Ministry at Bethany) that I was late because I had just come from visiting you. We had to pray and intercede for the persons whose hands we were holding. That's not coincidence. That's God's providence! Bishop did not preach. Instead, he notified the Church of his vision for the next 70 days. I took notes and printed them out for you, but I'm going to write them down here, in the body of this letter. I'm doing this because based on some things we've talked about during the visit, I think you might want to participate from where you are. You can even write down your prayer requests on a separate sheet of paper and ask Kelvin to lay it on the altar during Bible Study Wednesday nights. So, here is the outline:

For 30 days in August there will be corporate prayer, from 6:30 p.m. to 7:30 p.m. each Wednesday night. The congregation will enter the sanctuary, lay down their prayer requests, and pray at the altar. Bible Study will follow as usual, with special topics.

Every Tuesday night, from 7 p.m. to 8 p.m., the women will come together and pray.

Every Saturday night, from 7 p.m. to 8 p.m., the men will come together and pray.

Starting in September, there will be 40 days of prayer. More details will be given about the specifics.

I know there are no clocks around, but maybe you could ask a C.O. if they could tell you when it's 6:30 p.m. on Wednesdays and 7:00 p.m. on Saturdays so you can participate. Even if you don't write me a letter, write out your prayer requests (for yourself and others) and mail it out by Saturday or Monday to make sure it gets here by Wednesday. I think this would be great for you and what God is working out in your life right now. When we joined Bethany Baptist Church in Aug 2001 (10 years ago), I knew my/our destiny was tied to this Church. Now is an awesome and perfect opportunity for you to begin to manifest your destiny! My visit today was not an accident. It was all a part of God's plan! Since I can't be in Bible Study Wednesday nights, I'll get the CD and spend time on Thursdays listening, and taking notes, and mailing them out to you. You'll have time to study them and get your prayer requests written for the next week. Oh, God is so awesome! Who could have imagined that this would play out in this way, in this time of your life??? Nobody but God!

Continue to be encouraged, Justin. God has truly not forgotten you. Just believe that with all your being. Not because I say it, but because God has spoken it for you in His Word. He said, I will never leave you nor forsake you. You may have left and forsaken Him, but aren't you glad, He treats us better than we treat ourselves? I can't wait to see how you allow God to take over and use you for His glory. Not only once you come home, but while you are there. Obedience is better than sacrifice. Continue to obey and trust Him. He is your Heavenly Father and Creator. He knows you better than you know yourself.

I know this letter is full of thought-provoking challenges. You have the time and serenity to focus on them. Keep me posted on your progress.

I love you more than you could ever imagine. And yes, my chin is up.

Love you always, Mommie

August 2, 2011

Madre:

Ayo! What'z poppn' w/you? You really crusin' for a bruising! Where ma picturez at! SMH. I see how it iz mane. But you Gucci I don't want no problemz, Big Bruh.

I'm glad you and Joshua had a good visit. I enjoyed it myself. It waz nice to see you again. Wow, that'z really tha first time I saw someone I love in monthz. SMH. I need to get outta here! 77 dayz mane. Time is getting shorter every day. BTW, I came up with a nickname for Joshua. Imma call em Tazz when I get home. Reason bein', when he don't get hiz way, he start wildn' out like Tazz. I remember he used to do this spinnin' thing and would flap hiz handz in front of hiz chest. LOL. Dat kid crazy.

Mom I really am glad and grateful that you care about mhe and worry about mhe tha way you do, but sometimez I really wish you didn't. It aint fair that you go through any emotional pain cuz of my actionz. You didn't take ya motherz car and have thingz in there that you had no business havin'. You weren't on the edge of bein' Blood. You didn't commit a crime. So why should you suffer. I know you can't stop caring. Even if you want to. That'z one thing I've noticed. No matter how much you try to block out or ignore ya feelingz, they will still be there. An you still feel them. An no matter how well you may try and convince yourself you feel one way, you really feel another. The true feelin' iz what always comez out. I've learned to pay attention to dreamz. Dreamz are kinda like wishes ya heart desirez. And dreamz will also play a situation that involves ya true feeling. I just picked up on that thiz past week. Oh, I got a question, can tha devil attack uz through our dreamz? Like, put a lie of any kind in there? Something waz sed by someone else in a dream I had yesterday and it juz' made mhe wonder. But yeah, back to what I waz sayin', I feel so bad you gotta suffer cuz of mhe. Mom I'm truly, honestly and sincerely sorry for all thiz. I forgave myself. I hope you can to. I'm ready for the remaining 76 dayz to come. Rite now, I feel az tho I'm ready to come home, but to God I must not be cuz I'm still here. But when I do come home, thingz gone be different w/ mhe. You'll see.

I haven't told anybody thiz but, I'm so scared to come back. Meaning, if I don't go home on my recall, if I have like 11 or 10 monthz to a max, juz' the thought of bein' locked up that long, pluz the time I gotta do till October, iz really eatin' mhe up. I think I'd really have a nervous break-down. All tha stress I get now iz a lot. But for another year?

I couldn't do it. I'd really go crazy. I can't do thiz no more. I'm not built for thiz. I have to go home 10/18/11. I have to. I will. I know God will answer my prayer. I'm doing everything in my power to make sure that happen. I asked God to do what I can't, so I know I'll go home 10/18/11. Besidez, I really think I see Godz plan fallin' in place. And I keep passin' test after test. Yeah. I'm good. He'll get mhe home.

Thank you for the notez. I ain't read em yet, but I will when I start stressin' again. Imma let you know what I think about them.

Mr. Otis wrote mhe again. I like writing him. He'z very wize and he'z always tellin' mhe sumfin' that bringz understanding to mhe about sumfin'. SMH, that grammar waz bad. I juz' don't feel like scribblin'. But yeah, hiz letterz really encourage mhe. Thank you for giving him the address.

I want you to give mhe PopPopz address. I juz' wanna send sumfin' even if he don't write back. Tell him I miss him so much and I'm sorry for treatin him tha way I did. Let em know when I come home that will be different. Tell him and G-Ma I love em.

Well, ma wordz iz runnin' low. I'm tired & need to get these push-upz in before I go to sleep. So, imam holla at you when you write back, ya dig! BTW, I got my prayer request for next week. I'm not sure how to do it, so I'm juz' gonna take a shot at it. If itz wrong, tell mhe how to write it for next time. TTYL. Ma chin up Soldier. Stay strong!—JB

Prayer Request

I need prayer for myself. I need God to help mhe control my anger, so I don't let wordz be any more than what they are. I also need God to soften tha judgez heart towardz mhe when I go back to court in October. I need to go home. It iz not my destiny to be locked up.

Now I wanna ask for prayer for my girlfriend [Name]. I wanna ask God to take her stress. Keep her on point at all timez. Keep her happy and give her reasonz to laugh often. She has to endure pain threw my situation. I juz' wanna ask that God givez her hope, happiness and tha power to overcome what tha enemy throwz in her face.

I want God to bless my mother, Naomi. Give her strength and ease any storm in her heart. Let her unsettledness of her mind be settled. Give her happiness and tha power to overcome what tha enemy throwz in her face.

I want prayer for ma boyz, Ibn and Warren. Keep Ibnz mind settled. Give him a mature being. Help him be a leader and not a follower. Give him tha power to make hiz own decisionz. And God, give Warren hope & happiness.

Let him know that dayz will progress. No matter what. Even tho time for him iz long, it don't mean 'tz forever. Really God, give him hope. Bless hiz family. Keep strength in all their heartz.

Thursday, August 11, 2011

Mom,

Hey! I don't want you to write back to this. I juz' want you to read it and continue to pray for mhe az I do for myself. First, I have court this month on tha 18. IDK if you knew or not. But look, I'm beggin' you to please make sure you get there on time. I found out, I can't be released from court after my Judicial restriction date October 18. I been keepn' my faith strong and prayn' non-stop and I have a really strong feeling I may go home next week. I'll explain some stuff I waz lookin' at that makez mhe believe that.

All this iz from tha sermon notez.

-You must enter a season where you don't allow anyone or anything to hinder the move of God in your life.

So many people have been trying to get it in my head that I'm not going home any time soon. But I know that'z Satan tryin' to make mhe lose faith. But I refuse to do so.

-Don't disqualify yourself or you will miss your opportunity when it comes.

I have continued to stay charge free and not fite. August 18 iz my opportunity and I'm still in tha race.

-I am proof that God lives.

I asked God a long time ago to use mhe az an example of Hiz power. Seeing how thingz are playing out, it would make sense for mhe to go home in my situation.

-God will allow divine timing to be subject to man's activity.

That'z self- explanatory. God can overrule man.

-God is the ultimate opportunist. The same season He uses to produce dissatisfaction to produce change, is the same one He used to draw you closer to Himself.

Once again, self-explanatory.

-The working of the season is an act of destiny. Destiny will wake you up with a nightmare when you are in close proximity to its fulfillment.

Call it a fluke if you want, but ever since God opened my eyez wider, so I could see this plan, I've had nightmares every night since then. It iz my destiny to be home. It's coming soon.

I don't care if I look or sound stupid rite now, I got my faith in God . . . He really iz an awesome God! Don't tell anyone about this. Keep it to yourself. Pleaze, pleaze, pleaze make sure you and Uncle Brian are there. If either one of you haz anything planned, please cancel, or reschedule for mhe. I really don't want to miss this opportunity.

Mom. I'm so excited, even if I don't get to go home. My

time is getting short. My faith is unbreakable at this point. I give all my power and trust to God.

When we get in the courtroom, advocate for mhe. Talk about any progress you noticed & bring up Camden County College . . . Well, see you in a week! I love you—JB

Prayer Request

Mom

Hey! Thiz iz my prayer request for this week. Please ask Kelvin to put this on tha altar for mhe. If I didn't do it right can you rewrite it for mhe tha way itz supposed to be done, using what I sed? Thank you! I love you & I'll see you Thursday. I'm prayin' I come home. Pleaze do tha same. Bye! JB

-I would like to put a prayer request in for myself. I am in what I feel is tha worst storm of my life. Despite what man is telling me, God is putting an opportunity for tha storm to end earlier than what man wants it to. I have all my faith in God, but I just need a little extra prayer right now. I do not want my opportunity to go down tha drain. I continue to pray non-stop and ignore what the enemy is trying to do to throw mhe out of my walk w/God. All this is a lot on my heart and I need God to just touch my situation b/c I can't do it by myself.

-I would like to request prayer for a friend of mine named Warren. I know he has what he probably feels is unbearable stress on his shoulders. Just pray for him to let him know God is always there w/him & that he needs to keep his faith high no matter what. Let him know this is a

test and part of God's plan & that he will never put more on you than you can withstand. Let him know he needs to cry all tha tears necessary b/c tears are a sign of tha humble, not the weak.

God Bless!

Good morning Justin,

Sorry no hand-written letter this morning. I came down to the computer to print the sermon notes from last Sunday, Aug 14. I don't know if you recall or not but, August is always "Transforming Lives Month" at Bethany. We are supposed to bring someone to church every Sunday. Preferably, someone unsaved. Anyway, these sermons are geared toward the unsaved and encouraging them to accept Christ as their Savior and Lord.

I hope you can feel the passion in Bishop's voice as he preached this sermon through the words I have on the page. He spoke really quickly this time. I think I got the majority of the message. It speaks directly to your situation.

Also, Women of Judah is ministering to this Kurt Carr song, "Why Not Trust God Again" in service tomorrow. I so wish you could hear the music to go along with it. I'm not able to minister because I had to miss too many rehearsals with my trip to Cape Cod and being on call the following weekend. It really speaks to your personal situation; so, I wanted you to have the lyrics.

You have this great big picture of Joshua from the

computer. The color is not that great but . . . it's your brother. I'm going to CVS and print some others from my phone. I did what you suggested and emailed them to myself but, they are printing out too large and I don't know how to shrink them. If you don't see any regular 4x6s, then you'll know I had a little trouble and had to let it go and head to the post office before WOJ rehearsal.

Today is also the church picnic at Clementon Park. You know Kelvin has to be there to "volunteer." Joshua and I will go around 2:00 to be "participators." LOL, we like to have fun not work! Anyhow, I'll take pictures.

OK, Joshua is hungry and is asking for his mini pancakes. OMG, he's in the study saying, "Mommie, can you give me something to eat?" "Ok, Joshua." "Mommie, I'm really hungry," I gotta go. TTYL8R! Much Love, Smooches, Hugs and BIG KISSESS!!!!!!!!!—Mommie

Monday, September 5, 2011

2: *Mom*

From: JB33

Date: 9.5.11

Time: Getting shorter every day. 43 Dayz left

Hey Mom. Ther'z something I feel we need to discuss and I'd rather talk about it threw writing as we both can say everything we want to w/o getting interrupted. When I come home, I'm gonna be 17. I'm not a grown man yet, but Imma few 100 dayz away from it. When I waz home, you treated mhe like I was 13. I kinda think I have an idea on why you did that & you can correct mhe if I'm wrong. For a very long time it waz juz' you and mhe. I was ya everything. Well I hope I still am. But az I got older, deep down you really didn't wanna let mhe grow up, which caused you to treat mhe younger than my age. Well Mom, when I come home, I would like to be treated like I'm 17. Next year Imma be a grown man. And when I was home, you waz giving mhe early, unreasonable curfewz, taking my phone, SMH. I know I waz actin' like a (fool) before I got locked up, but that waz then. I told [my girlfriend] the same thing. I'm

more mature now and all that young kid stuff that waz hap-
pinin' iz out tha window. So, since I am deciding to act my
age, I'm expecting to be treated my age. I don't mean to come
off w/ so much hostility w/thiz, but if you try to do what
you waz doin' when I waz home, we are never gonna have
a happy household. I wanted to write this, so you could have
some time to prepare for when I come home. We can have
a good relationship Mom. If you work w/mhe, I'll work w/
you, so just keep that in mind.

Well that'z all I gotta say for now. If this feelz like I'm
commin' off w/negative feelinz, just ignore it cuz that'z not
my intentionz, ite? Imma save some love for tha next letter,
ya dig!

I love you!—JB

Monday, September 12, 2011

Hey Justin,

Sorry our last phone call was not the best. I just don't want you slipping back to your old way of thinking. I've been so proud of the progress you've been making. I don't want you to lose momentum. You are too close to possibly coming home to have a setback now.

I should have gotten these sermon notes out to you sooner. Perhaps they could have been a help to you. Stay encouraged Justin. Your time is much too short to mess up now. I know you have a roommate, but you still need to meditate on these notes. I know they will be strength to your spirit and food to your soul.

I love you much and will never give up on you.

TTYL8R-Mommie

*This letter smells like me. It's Coach. You like it???☺

2: *Mom*

From: JB33

Date: 9.14.11

Hey Mom, I really needed thoze notez you sent. Satan is really tryna get mhe messed up. He knoz I only have to make it one more month and he keepz makin' it difficult for mhe to stay on tha right track. I almost did something so stupid. So, so, so stupid and it waz really nothing but God getting mhe out of that situation. Mom, I've been slipping w/God, mainly cuz I have a roommate and I can't talk to Him how I used to cuz I don't have the privacy. But I still find a little time to pray. Mom, please just don't stop praying for mhe. I need God to take 100% control cuz I cannot do it by myself. I feel weak and down right now. I feel alone and scared. I wanna go home so bad. And when I sed I feel weak, down, alone, and scared, I meant ma spirit. I'm alrite physically, but ma mind and spirit iz in a war rite now. I'm struggling w/pride rite now. In all honesty, I wish I could juz' run into ya armz and have you tell mhe everything iz okay & you

make it all go away. I hate this jail life man. Jus please keep
prayin' for mhe Mom. Pleaze.

Well, I love you Mom. I hope you stayin' stronger than
I am. Stay safe—JB

Tuesday, September 20, 2011

2: *Mom*

From: JB33

Date: 9.20

Time: Getting Real Short

Mood: On Point

Well, I got some stuff to tell you and I don't want you to start trippin' cuz I'm still gonna come home in 28 dayz. It feels so good to say I got four weekz left. Anyway, some fake, tuff (Dude) got embarrassed when he tried to play mhe in front of ma boyz. I guezz his pride got hurt so he felt he needed to redeem himself by poppn' on mhe. Mom, I been restrainin' myself to tha point where (Dudes) waz sayin' (f) my mother, inviting mhe to their privatez and juz' talkin' all crazy. I never popped, I juz' swallowed my pride and let 10-18 be my motivation. But he put hiz handz on mhe, so you can't be mad at mhe. Tha CO that workz tha pod knowz my situation and iz lookin' mhe out. The way he wrote tha charge should benefit mhe (institutional charge). He also told mhe juz' tell tha judge I grabbed him, so he couldn't swing no more and it turned into a wrestle on tha floor. But the COz still had to write it up as a fight. So, I still have faith that God iz gonna pull mhe through this.

Now, they put mhe in the box for two dayz, so I came out yesterday. Now, I'm on C-Level till Monday and I'll go back to Population then. But anyway, Ibn got put on C-Level last nite too. Some (gang members) jumped him and some other (kids) from (city). Now, I'm the only one from Camden County in the Pod and there'z like six Middlesex (dudes). They wanna jump mhe cuz of where I'm from and they know I'm by myself. That would never happen in Pop cuz they scared of ma boyz. But that aint tha case. Now, I swallowed my pride and put myself on the upper tier so we not in tha same group. So now, I just gotta relax until Monday and hope they don't catch mhe by myself. Cuz, if you get jumped by more than three ppl, they give you a riot charge and I definitely won't go home. If I don't fight back, they might knock mhe out or break something cuz itz 6 of them. But I'm juz' hopin' I get back around tha homiez before anything dumb happenz.

28 days seemz so long, but so short. Like, I remember when I thought I wasn't cumin home till next year. Now, itz less than a month. I really learned ma lesson. Thiz iz really what I needed. I ain't seen no one I love except you and ma Dad for the past five monthz. SMH. I really ain't built for this & I swear to God you'd find mhe dead before you find mhe locked up again. Imma keep prayin' God givez mhe grace, mercy, and uncommon favor.

Stay strong Mom. Write back ASAP Ya dig!!

I Love you!—JB

PS: Make sure you come up here on ma birthday. 12 dayz till I'm 17!

Saturday, September 24, 2011

Hi Justin!

I'm sitting in the sanctuary at church writing you today. I just finished WOJ dance rehearsal and wanted to make sure I got this letter done to mail by noon today.

I must tell you how absolutely relieved I was to have had the opportunity to talk to you last night. I was so concerned about your mental and spiritual wellbeing. I and the women in WOJ have been praying earnestly for your sense of peace and right mindedness.

I know you have a roommate now, but Justin, you have to stay prayed up and meditating on the sermon notes and letters you've received from your loved ones thus far. You cannot make it through this test and trial without God's strength. If you want to hear His voice and what He has to say to you, you must spend time with Him. Are you able to go to your room at any time or only when you're told? Perhaps you can carve out a certain time of day to spend in prayer and meditation.

The newest thing we are doing at Bethany is 40 days of prayer. Remember I told you we were moving on to that? I've sent you your very own journal. Once again, God's timing is never accidental. This journal came out just when you needed it. Each day has a scripture focus, a short thought for the day, and space for you to write your personal thoughts/prayers. I'm going to start mine on October 1. I'd like you to do the same. What an awesome way for us to prepare for your upcoming court appearance!! If you are trusting God to do great things, to show you uncommon favor, and move the heart of the judge, then place your prayer focus on those things. Still continue to consider your future and what you need to do in the weeks after you come home. Satan is going to be busy in your head, heart, and body. You cannot allow him to penetrate those areas that God should be protecting. You must stay prayed up and focused forward.

I have read your letter, as I told you when we spoke. The second letter, I've not yet seen. I am coming to see you on your birthday. I've not decided whether or not to bring Joshua. I don't think I want him to see all the inmates in a common room like that. He may have too many questions I'm not willing to address during our visit time. If Kelvin wants to come, then Joshua will come.

Ok. Imma go now to get to the post office on time. Love you much and see you real soon.

Smooches and Hugs—Love, Mommie

Monday, September 26, 2011

2: Mom

From: JB33

Date: 9.26.11

Time: 22 Days left, something lite

What'z good Ma? I got your letter today. I hear what you sayin' about stayin' close to God. Since I got moved to C-Level, I don't have a roommate anymore. I still pray and I continue to ask for grace, mercy, and uncommon favor. With all that'z happened, honestly, I realli don't think imma go home. Based off of logic. But, what makez mhe believe imma go home iz that God haz promised mhe victory. I just have to go through tha storm. My faith iz high and that'z where itz stayin'. I proved to myself that I'm stronger minded now. You can even ask [my girlfriend]. I'm more mature in my actionz and thought process. I've learned how to respond rather than react or retaliate. I'm, well, I tried to get everything I need to stay home. I know I have what it takez now. My main problem waz not thinking and just doing and anybody can see I've got way better control over that. I'm readi to come home. I know God is using these final weekz to test what he'z made of mhe and I refuse to fail. Imma see you on the outside real soon.

I can't believe I have three weeks left. Time went by so fast once I got to 60 dayz. I remember 4.18 I was sick az a dog! Now, I'm on ma way out again. I promise to you, I promised to [my girlfriend], and I promised to myself that I'm done w/jail. I can't come back and I won't.

Well, I can't wait to see you Sunday. I can't believe I'm turning 17 in prison. SMH. Oh well. Get mhe tha iPhone from Verizon when I come home ☺ LOL, Thatl be a good present. But anyway three weekz iz something light. Juz' eat that up real quick and I'll be home. See you soon!

I love you!—JB

DEVOTIONAL ANECDOTE:

A LESSON FROM ACHSAH

†

The story of Achsah is of a woman who wanted more.
Joshua 15:16–19

The territories around the people of Judah were determined by their families.

Joshua gave Caleb a portion of Judah called Hebron. From there he drove out the three sons of Anak. Then he marched against the people living in Kiriath Sepher. Caleb said, "I will give my daughter Achsah in marriage to the man who attacks and captures the enemy stronghold of Kiriath Sepher." Othniel captured it and was given Achsah in marriage.

One day when she came to her husband, she urged him to ask her father for a field. She rode up to Caleb and dismounted her donkey. He asked her what she wanted, and she replied, "Do me a special favor. Since you have given me the land of the Negev, give me also springs of water." So he gave her the upper and the lower springs.

As a portion of her dowry, Achsah was given a portion in the desert of Israel's south district. The region receives very little rain due its extreme temperatures and its location to the east of the Sahara, as opposed to the Mediterranean, which lies to the west. It only receives an average of twenty-four millimeters of rainfall per year. Though appreciative of her gift, Achsah was not content. She wanted springs of water to irrigate the fields so that the land would be fruitful. He gave her a double portion of what she asked for; the upper and lower springs, thereby assuring her success. Isn't that just like a good father?

"Boldness is a great virtue, but it does not begin on the battlefield or in the midst of great conflict. Our boldness must begin in our prayer life. (Grady 2012, 78).

The prayer for "uncommon favor" was one of boldness toward supernatural provision; for a dry and thirsty area in Justin's life to be watered by the One who is the Living Water. Our prayer was for a double portion of His blessing. We were bold enough to ask God for more. We understood that Christ dwells in our hearts by faith and that the depths of His love for us are boundless. We found ourselves in a safe place where we were watered emotionally and spiritually. We were not left barren, brittle, and scorned in the desert sun of our circumstances.

Psalm 91 became Justin's banner. He dwelt in the secret place of the Most High and rested under the shadow of the Almighty. He proclaimed God as his refuge and fortress and put his trust in Him. He was delivered from the hand of the dangerous enemy. He was covered by God's feathers and found refuge under His wings. God's faithfulness became his shield and defense. He was not afraid of the terror by night; nor of the arrow that flew by day; nor the enemy that stalked in darkness; nor the affliction that destroyed by midday. One thousand may have fallen by his side and ten thousand by his right hand, but it did not come near him. He observed the punishment of the wicked with his own eyes. Since he said "the Lord is my refuge," and he made the Most High his dwelling place, no harm overtook him, and no disaster came near his cell. God's angles were commanded concerning Justin, and they guarded him in all of his ways. They lifted Justin up in their hands, so that he would not strike his foot against a stone. He has the ability to tread on the lion and cobra; and trample the young lion and any mythical monster. The Lord has said, because Justin loves Me and acknowledges My name, I will rescue and protect him. He called on Me and I answered. I will be with him in trouble, deliver him, and honor him. I will satisfy him with long life and show him My salvation.

As a mother trusting God to be what I could not; strength when I was weak; vision when my sight was dim; peace in the midst of the storm; and courage when I was fainthearted; I found solace in the truth of Deuteronomy 32:10–12:

"In the dessert land he found him, in a barren and howling waste. He shielded him and cared for him; he guarded him as the apple of his eye, like an eagle that stirs up its nest and hovers over its young, that spreads its wings to catch them and carries them aloft. The Lord alone led him; no foreign god was with him."

Do not underestimate God's ability to bless you. Approach boldly and ask *big*!

QUESTIONS TO CONSIDER

1. What area of your life needs the covering of God's uncommon favor?
2. To whom do you need to write letters from your heart?
3. How can you encourage yourself to trust God?
4. How can you encourage your child or others to trust God?

WORDS OF ENCOURAGEMENT

"There has never been a storm that didn't water the ground."—Bishop David G. Evans

SONG FOR YOUR SEASON

"Why Not Trust God Again"—Kurt Carr

ACT OF KINDNESS

Find something positive to say about your child every day.

†
Uncommon Favor

*T*his iz the last night I'm sleepin' in thiz bed; in thiz cell between theze four grey concrete wallz. I'm so excited I can't sleep. Quite a few inmates are telling mhe I'm not goin' home, but I don't believe them. I refuse to believe them. I shout encouragin' wordz through the ventz to Chris in the cell next door because he iz goin' home on parole. But mhe? I lay here alone believin' God will make a way. That He will grant mhe "uncommon favor" and allow the judge to send mhe home on a recall tomorrow.

I wake at 4 am like I ain't here. Az if I'm already home. I start packin' up my personal itemz explainin' to the C.O.z that I ain't comin' back. Even they are tellin' mhe I'm not goin' home, but man, I feel so light on the inside. I'm puttin' on thiz tan jumpsuit and eatin' breakfast here for the last time.

They shackle and load mhe into the back of a paddy wagon. There'z not one negative thought in my mind, juz' relief. I'm all alone and ridin' to my freedom. I'm one step *closer to home. All I can think about iz gettin' my life back; seein' my mom, my 'lil brotha, and the rest of my family; holdin' my girlfriend; and doin' what I want when I want.*

The one-hour drive seemed so short. The driver pulled up to the back of the courthouse and ushered mhe out. Oh my God. I'm finally here! Man, thiz iz real!

That was the day that the Lord had made. I would rejoice and be glad in it!

Lord, I have fasted, prayed, trusted, and believed. Today is the day I trust You to show Yourself sovereign once again in the courtroom. Dispatch Your angles before us to set the atmosphere. Let every word spoken be according to Your will for the fulfillment of Your Word concerning Justin. Let no man get the glory that is due Your name. Humble our hearts. Steady our minds. Calm our spirits. Settle our thoughts on You and You alone. Our thoughts and ways are not Yours. Help us to receive and accept Your expressed will for this day. May Your will, not ours, be done. Give us an opportunity to bless Your name and praise You for the good that will come of this hearing. You are and always will be in complete control. We have prayed for Your uncommon favor and expect nothing less than for You to deliver. This is our heart's desire and I humbly ask that it be granted. In Jesus's name, Amen.

These last six months had been a paradoxical blessing. Though Justin had been in custody outside the home, my heart had been at peace, knowing he was safe, but I was concerned for his emotional and physical well-being. I've asked myself, "Why don't I hear his music? Why don't I hear him rapping? He's not dead. Why isn't he here?" How can it be that a mother's heart could ache and still experience peace at the same time?

Kelvin's and my marriage had grown stronger and closer without the daily angst of two males seeking to territorialize one home. Now that the day had come, I cautiously proceeded with considerable apprehension.

I was ecstatic to realize Kelvin would be by my side in court that day. God had softened his heart toward this entire situation, and for that, I was grateful. We ate breakfast, dropped Joshua off at day care, and drove that all too familiar route to the courthouse.

This time, I was a passenger reveling in the opportunity to sit quietly with my eyes closed and my mind focused. Gone were the anxiety and agony over the inevitable separation of a mother from her child. In its place was the confident peace of the hopeful reunion of a mother with her son. Yet, in the recesses of my mind lay the dreadful possibility of him being sent back. *Lord,*

you never put more on me than I can bear. Please carry the
weight of this burdensome thought on your shoulders.

Upon our arrival to the hallway, we were met, as usual, by my brother Brian. We greeted Justin's additional support team of his father; Aunt Jamila; and paternal grandmother, Carolyn, with hugs and well wishes. Prayerfully, for the final time, we entered the courtroom.

October 19, 2011

"We're here on a recall that I called," said the judge.

The prosecutor responded, "The state's position at this particular point is that the disposition should stand. The juvenile did not get any additional time for additional offenses on a negotiated agreement based on the fact that he was already incarcerated, then used that disposition period to ask for a recall on what he was already serving. It just seems a little backward to the state that he would get lesser time when he came for more offenses. That being said, it is my understanding that the juvenile did have a parole board hearing on the twenty-fifth, or at least one was scheduled, and I don't know what the result of that was, but, at this point, the state's position is that we should leave it in the hands of the parole board. I don't know if they set a date for him. I don't have that information."

"I know the history of the case. We've lived it. Here's what I'm interested in: you're on a recall. Everything that you're talking about up until I sent him away is why he's away. I'm interested in what's going on now. If you want to address me that's fine. But I'm gonna want to hear from him too," said the judge.

Brian stepped in. "Judge, you have received two letters with Justin expressing himself. And I can state that throughout this time period, I thought that it was a difficult road to rehabilitation for Justin, and unfortunately for him, I thought that he was just beginning to demonstrate genuine remorse and acceptance of responsibility, and growth and maturity, from the events at the time around the sentencing; and that may have factored into the court's willingness to do a recall in six months. Since that time, I can tell you, I have been very much impressed with Justin's evolution. As expressed, I don't have a copy of the letter from August because I got it that day, but I do have a copy of the one that I faxed to Your Honor more recently. And in Justin's words, and I do think this is sincere, he says,

"'Your Honor, (with respect to today's date), please send me home today. I know I am ready to handle freedom. I've had so much time to mature and put myself in the mindset I need to begin to succeed as an African American male and to change society. I stated before, I am not a heartless gangbanger. These six months away from home really paid me with a reality check. I'm not going to try and manipulate your decision with a bunch of reasons why I think I should go home. If you go shopping, you can see that talk is still cheap. I need the opportunity to show everyone, and myself, what I can accomplish at my full potential.'

And he goes on to thank Your Honor for his consideration. That last part of what he said, 'Everyone and myself,' I think that Justin finally has gotten it. Man, he dealt with a lot of anger and emotional issues with circumstances going on in his home that are beyond his ability to control. I think he's worked very hard over the years to resolve those issues with various therapists at different times. Also, he has gotten to a much better point with his mother and with his stepfather, who are present in court today, and also his natural father is up from DC today. And again, I know the more serious offenses he committed were eluding the police, but I think on the backdrop of some of the emotional and health issues that Justin has struggled with, I think that what he's really failed to control were his impulses.

"He has a lot of issues with pride. And when he felt his pride was violated, it would trigger his anger and impulsive behavior, and Justin struggled with really controlling that. He has been prescribed medication to help him deal with the defiance disorder that he developed. I think that this time in custody, with the nature of the environment there, the challenges that he was presented with, I think that, that in and of itself, shows that he just has not retaliated. He has been challenged every day. And, if Your Honor recalls his letter from August, he spoke very vividly about how he felt like a punk, and how he felt like less than a man, and how everyone was challenging him, and he was not going to do anything to blow his top in there and retaliate. And, I think, Your Honor, when he left that day, Your Honor said, 'That's exactly what I'm looking for in October.'

"And I knew his emotional and mental state at that time, I was somewhat concerned. He was crying because he had a fear of going back down there. He did not think he would survive another day, and yet he has gone on to survive another sixty days, and now stands before the court in a more stable emotional condition in that regard.

"And I think also important to note, not only the circumstances of these challenges, these things he struggled to deal with in regard to his own emotional makeup, he's done this without the benefit of therapy or medication, judge. So he has demonstrated that he has the ability to control his anger; to control his impulses, even without that assistance. Again, Your Honor, I think that Justin finally gets it. He has finally gotten it. And that for some people, you know, you have to really hit rock bottom before you get it.

"I'll state this very briefly, in representing my nephew, and the court knows he's my nephew, I've had to look at myself, you know, twenty years removed. A lot of the issues that Justin struggles with, anger and impulsive behavior, I struggled with on my own. And I had a lot of bad experiences in my life consequentially, but, fortunately for me, I did not have to go to a place like Jamesburg to finally get it. I fought like hell, like a lot of other people in my family. A lot of services were available to help Justin avoid that reality for himself. He made the bed, he had to lie in it, and he's done it.

When I went to talk to him at the JMSF, I said, 'Listen, man, I'm really sorry you had to experience the transfer from Jamesburg to JMSF. I wish you would have had the chance to do the programs the court committed you to do, so this experience could have been as soft as it could have been for you.' Justin said to me, 'Nah, I needed it just like this for me to really get it. Like I needed to feel it exactly as I've been feeling it here.' I trust and believe and hope that Justin really has gotten it. And if Your Honor believes that that's true, then I respectfully ask the court to consider maybe a change of the sentence, maybe to a time served with probation with whatever conditions going forward the court might consider."

"Do you want to address me?" the judge asked Justin.

"Yeah, bro. About the whole pride issue. That was my main issue going in there, pride. Like, when I first went down there, it was a big issue to swallow my pride. But being down there I learned how to do that. I think that's what I need to learn how to do on the streets too. I need to swallow my pride. That's a lot of the reason why I was getting in trouble too. But . . ."

"I read your letters, Justin. Is there anything else you want to tell me?"

"Yes, I really think I rehabilitated myself without all that counseling, with just the time in there, sitting there reflecting on my life in my cell."

"What meds are you on?"

"I'm not on anything right now."

"No meds at all? All right, anything else? If any of

the family wants to speak, I'll address that. But I don't believe I need to hear from them."

Brian chimed in. "I was just going to ask. I don't know if his mother wanted to speak. He has a commitment to get back to school and she looked into a couple different programs for him. I didn't know if Your Honor . . ."

"No. I don't need to hear that. I know this is a committed family, committed to his education and the like. Justin had a rough road. Justin, I'm going to cut to the chase. I am going to change your sentence to time served. And, I'm going to give you probation henceforth; so, you're going be released. I commend you for what you've done. I looked at the report from August 22. I could have waited longer. I understand what the state said, leave it up to the parole board, etc. But there comes a time where I'm weighing the talent that this young man has as opposed to keeping him in Jamesburg, which, in some respect, becomes a trap for him."

The judge continued, "Six months is no short time for a seventeen-year-old boy. Six months is a lifetime, and he's been there that long; and he has made substantial, impressive adjustments. He's negotiated positive movement into the less restrictive areas of JMSF. I'm going to read from the report:

"'Both pod officers report he has been quiet and respectful, and his peer relationships are fine. He's been meticulous regarding personal hygiene, and maintains a neat and clean, living space.'

"I understand you had a couple of institutional offenses. I expected it to be much worse. I understand he's going to need aggression replacement training. As part of his probation, this court is going to require that he has continued anger management therapy, okay, as part of it because I think that's necessary. I think he will need that support. Because you have chosen to step away from even the medications, and do it on your own. . . . You know, you can continue to take pills every day, but someday, you will get tired of taking the pills, or if the pills lose their effectiveness, you're not any better than the day you started taking them. But, if you do it without the pills, then you've done it. You've accomplished it and you don't need anybody except yourself waking up in the morning to address your issues every day. And as a young man, you realize that you can do it; that's why I'm going in this direction.

"I believe at this point, the mitigating factors do outweigh the aggravating factors in terms of a change in the sentence. Because I believe, that there is now, at this point in time, a substantial likelihood that he will be particularly able to respond affirmatively to probationary treatment in a noncustodial sentence. He has taken serious steps to prevent the type of conduct, which resulted in delinquent acts, from happening again. He is smart enough. And that's the other thing. This is a young man that's reading on a twelfth-grade level at Jamesburg. I am not going to torture that mind in that setting, because I could lose it at some point. If I keep him there, I'll just be setting a trap for him to mess up, because I'm what? Punishing him? My purpose for sending him there was to see if he could turn around. Six months is a long time. It's not a short period of time and he's taken advantage of the opportunity. The other thing that can't go without saying is that he has a supportive family structure that's going to be there for him. His family really cares about him.

"You understand that, son?"

"Yeah."

"Because that's who you're throwing away. Now, you're willing to embrace it again because you're going to need that family structure when you get out. Understand that I'm saying a lot of nice things about you at this point in time because you deserve to hear them. You worked your way back from being a delinquent to being potentially a very productive member of our society.

"I am converting the sentence to probationary term along with the time that you served. However, you're on probation. You mess up on probation, son, and I skip right ahead to all the little interim steps that didn't work for you, and I put you right back where you were. Do you understand?"

"Yeah."

"Because it's easy. It's shorthand, then. I knew all the stuff that didn't work. All the nonsense stuff that didn't work for you before. I won't start at the bottom again. If I let you go home on probation, and you mess up, it's your ticket right back to where you're telling me you don't ever want to be again. That should be enough motivation to keep you on the straight and narrow. You think?"

"I know."

"Okay, good. Counsel, the term of probation is going to be until his nineteenth and a half birthday, which is April 2, 2014. Until you're nineteenth and a half, you're going be on probation, son. Understand?"

"Yeah."

"All right, Justin, good luck, and trust me, I'm the only guy that's gonna be here until you're nineteenth and a half, so it's you and me. You asked me to be 'warm in my heart,' so to speak in the letter; I'm not. I'm not. I'm just fair. And, what's fair is fair. I put a test to you, and you passed the test. Now if you come out, and you fail the next test, you go back in. It's that simple with me."

"All right."

"Understood?"

"Yeah."

"All right, very good."

"Thank you very much again, Your Honor," Brian remarked.

"You're welcome, counsel. Thank you for the manner in which you represented him."

"Appreciate it."

Adjourned.

And just like that! My overwhelmed heart was overjoyed! When the judge said, "Justin, I'm going to cut to the chase. I am going to change your sentence to time served. You're going to be released," my head fell into my lap and I began to sob. The heavy weight of anticipation that draped my entire being was lifted. All the months of praying, writing encouraging letters, and believing against all the odds that God's uncommon favor would reign supreme had come to pass. My breathing was labored and swift. My heart, racing and pounding. My hands, shaking and sweating—not because my son is running through the woods, but because he was coming home!

I heard, "Keeping him in Jamesburg becomes a trap for him" and "You asked me to be warm in my heart, I'm not. I'm just fair. I put a test to you, and you passed the test. I'm saying a lot of nice things about you because you deserve to hear them." Like, what judge says that?

It's as if the remainder of the hearing happened in slow motion. I was so happy, my insides were fluttering. I walked over to Justin and hugged him shackled in that tan jumpsuit for the very last time. He was taken to the back while we exited the courtroom into the hallway.

Oh what joy! What an occasion for celebration. We hugged and sighed and laughed and cried. Tears of deliverance flowed freely down my face. The next step was determining when, and how, he would be released into my custody.

I feel an overwhelmin' amount of relief and happiness. I am ready for a new beginnin'. I can't wait to see my girlfriend.

"Mom!" I heard Justin's voice far behind me. Turning around, he was running toward me in an off-white, long-sleeve, thermal shirt, with a six-digit state-issued number across the left upper chest; light gray cotton shorts; white sweat socks; and tan construction boots. I could not believe my eyes. "What is this? How are you out here?"

"I'm released! I'm free! They can't hold me anymore."

"Where's all your belongings?"

"Right here. I got all my letterz in here. They only allowed me two big envelopez with all my stuff. I kept all the letterz you and [my girlfriend] wrote mhe, but I had to give all the sermon notez away."

"What? Why did you have to give them away? They were an important part of your journey. They have sentimental value."

"Itz all right, Mom. I gave them to my boyz who I know could benefit from them. I got what I needed from them. I can go to church and hear Bishop for myself. There'z dudez in there that can't do that. They need them more than I do. Itz all good."

"Where are your clothes?"

"I don't have none. Thiz iz all I got to my name."

"What about the ones you wore goin' in?"

"Mom, I don't know, and I don't care. I'm good. I got clothez on and I'm outta here. Letz go!"

A LESSON FROM MARY, THE MOTHER OF JESUS
†

The story of Mary is one of obedience and surrender.
Luke 1:26–38 (NIV)

In the sixth month of Elizabeth's pregnancy, God sent the angel Gabriel to Nazareth, a town in Galilee, to a virgin pledged to be married to a man named Joseph, a descendant of David. The virgin's name was Mary. The angel went to her and said, "Greetings, you who are highly favored! The Lord is with you."

Mary was greatly troubled at his words and wondered what kind of greeting this might be. But the angel said to her, "Do not be afraid, Mary; you have found favor with God. You will conceive and give birth to a son, and you are to call him Jesus. He will be great and be called the Son of the Most High. The Lord God will give him the throne of his father David, and he will reign over Jacob's descendants forever; his kingdom will never end."

"How will this be," Mary asked the angel, "since I am a virgin?"

The angel answered, "The Holy Spirit will come on you, and the power of the Most High will overshadow you. So the holy one to be born will be called the Son of God. Even Elizabeth, your relative, is going to have a child in her old age, and she who was said to be unable to conceive is in her sixth month. For no word from God will ever fail."

"I am the Lord's servant," Mary answered. "May your word to me be fulfilled." Then the angel left her.

Though not pregnant with the Messiah, I had much in common with Mary.

I was the perfect, unlikely choice when God sent His angel to speak into my spirit. I would give birth as an unmarried Christian woman in medical school, fulfilling His calling: *Greetings! You who are highly favored, the Lord is with you. Be not troubled. You have found favor with God. You will conceive and bear a son and call his name Justin. He will be great.*

I was pregnant with purpose and promise.

I was a willing servant who, through an act of sinful disobedience, continued to trust God and obey His call. The joys of motherhood are deeply woven with great pains in the privilege of being Justin's mother. I was a woman of courage and character who loved God and wanted to serve Him with all my heart.

"(I) was willing to surrender (my) life to the will of God no matter the cost to (my) family or reputation. We must come to a place where we can say with Mary, 'May it be done to me according to Your word'" (Grady 2012, 151, 154).

1. What area in your life has required gut-wrenching surrender?
2. How has that act of obedience affected your walk of faith?
3. How have you used your blessings to bless others?
4. What does God's uncommon favor look like in your life?

WORDS OF ENCOURAGEMENT

Favor does not eliminate the process.

SONG FOR YOUR SEASON

"Let Go"—DeWayne Woods

ACT OF KINDNESS

Surrender one thing that prevents you from experiencing God's uncommon favor.

CHAPTER EIGHT

†

Just Breathe

I don't feel no ways tired,
I've come too far from where
I started from
Nobody told me that
the road would be easy,
I don't believe He's brought me this far
to leave me

—James Cleveland

September 2019

Who said I would have a fabulous life with a husband, three kids, and a home surrounded by a white picket fence?

Who said my children would attend private school, play musical instruments, and speak foreign languages?

Who said my son would love school, graduate with honors, and have his pick of undergraduate universities?

Who said my buttons would pop and my cheeks burn every time his name was mentioned?

Who said my son would be well-groomed and be remarkably sought after for his golden skin, long locs, and prominent cheekbones?

Who said? Was it me? Were those my thoughts? Did I treasure those somewhere deep within my heart? Had I not been entitled to those realities? Had I not sacrificed? Had I not struggled? Had I not suffered? Surely I was owed.

There must have been some mistake.

Oh, now I see. I was a good Christian girl. Obedient. A follower of the rules. Seeking Him for direction. Fulfilling His will for my life. But then it happened. You know. Well, I was disobedient. I conceived and bore a son out of wedlock. I would carry my "issue" before me in plain sight. The scarlet letter across my chest displayed more vividly than the humbled heart beneath it.

So, this was it? That was my reward? The consequence for my disobedience? Okay, I got it. I could shoulder this. I could make this work.

Then the voice of the Lord spoke to me through His Word:

"Not so, my child. That is not my voice. I love you so much that I gave my only Son for your sake. My thoughts are not your thoughts nor my ways your ways. I know the thoughts that I think toward you. They are of peace and not of evil, to give you a future and a hope. Many are the afflictions of the righteous, but I will deliver you from them all. Come unto me, all who are weary and heavy laden, and I will give you rest. Take my yoke upon you, learn of me, for I am meek and lowly in heart. You will find rest for your soul. My yoke is easy, and my burden is light. Nothing can separate you from my love. And as for Ishmael (Justin), I have heard you; I have blessed him and will make him fruitful. I will multiply him exceedingly" (John 3:16; Isaiah 55:8; Jeremiah 29:11; Psalm 34:19; Matthew 11:28–30; Romans 8:28; Genesis 17:20).

Hiding God's Word in your heart not only helps you obey Him, but through worship and prayer, you will develop a strong, meaningful, reciprocal relationship with Him. Spending sacred time with Him sharpens your ear to distinguish His voice from any other. Over time, the result of that nurturing produces the fruit of the Spirit, which is love, joy, peace, long-suffering, gentleness, goodness, faith, meekness, and temperance (Galatian 5:22–23). Possessing this fruit is like a ballast for your soul.

A ballast is a heavy material—such as gravel, sand, iron, or lead—placed low in a vessel to improve its stability in the water. Its weight is greater than the weight of the boat on top. Don't get so bogged down with what's going on in the external parts of your life. If your ballast is built up with prayer, praise, and worship, you will possess the fruit of the Spirit. When the storms of life rage, you'll possess the weight of the ballast beneath to weather the storm above.

Take refuge in these words penned by Douglas Miller:

"Though the storms keep on raging in my life . . . my soul has been anchored in the Lord."

Nicodemus was a Pharisee. He was a ruler of the Jewish sect that flourished during the first century BCE and the first century AD. The Pharisees strictly observed religious ceremonies and practices, adhered to oral laws and traditions, and believed in an afterlife and the coming of a messiah.

In John, Chapter 3, he came to Jesus by night acknowledging his position as rabbi and teacher come from God. But he was puzzled when Jesus replied that a man cannot see the Kingdom of God except he be born again. Nicodemus asked the obvious: "How can a man be born when he is old? Can he enter a second time into his mother's womb and be born?" Jesus answered: "Except a man be born of the water and Spirit, he cannot enter into the Kingdom of God. That which is born of flesh is flesh;

and that which is born of Spirit is spirit." Nicodemus continued to ponder the answer.

No, I could not enter a second time into my mother's womb to be reborn, but I could enter again into His presence to be reborn in the Spirit. I attended Hawa Jusu Johnson's Living Empowered women's retreat at Sandy Cove Ministries in northeast, Maryland. The theme was "Reset!" and my expressed goal was for realignment. As I lay faceup on a yoga mat, the following was what I experienced through guided imagery lead by Bernai Holman from Go Strong Fitness:

"Pay attention to the filling and emptying of your lungs.

"Inhale for three. Exhale for three.

"Your encounter and acceptance with Him give you access to enter a beautiful relationship with Him. One that you can bask in right now.

"Inhale for four. Exhale for four.

"Your faith gives you authority to walk with Him; to know Him better, to love Him better, and to furthermore feel His love for you.

"Inhale for five. Exhale for five.

"As we get to bigger breaths, allow yourself to melt into the ground.

"Beginning with your head. Allow your hair to relax on either side. Sink your head, allowing your brain to shut off from the hustle and bustle of the to-do list. No list today. No duties today. Just a meeting in a free space where you can be authentically you. A time that is unhindered and an opportunity to be in God's presence to hear an authentic word.

"Allow your shoulders to melt into the floor. Take the weight off. Take the expectations off.

"Matthew 28:30 says, 'Come to Me all who labor and are heavy laden and I will give you rest. Take My yoke upon you and learn from Me for I am gentle and lowly in heart and you will find rest for your souls for My yoke is easy and My burden is light.'

"Feel the release. We have to release in order to receive. In this moment, there is no expectation of you. Just be. Just breathe. Just inhale and exhale. Release and embrace. Let go and accept.

"Inhale for six and exhale for six.

"As you do this, place your hand on your heart. Be thankful that you can feel your heartbeat, which means your purpose is living inside of you. Destiny is waiting for you, and life is gifted to you.

"Place your hands on your ears. Be thankful that

you can hear God when He speaks. Allow your thoughts to quiet. The doubts to shut off. The fears to be erased. Come empty to Him and ready to be filled with God's Word and His promises.

"Inhale for seven. Exhale for seven.

"Allow your heart to relax. Muscles are being repaired and mended. It happens best when we are at rest. Allow for one moment in time to not feel obligated to hurt because of your past, to hurt because of your mistakes, or hurt because someone decided to treat you like you were less of a royal priesthood; the royal priesthood that God created you to be. Or to hurt because God decided something different than what you expected. That hurt created calluses in your heart. That's what makes it difficult to allow the good in. You must release it. Add water to your heart and wash away the pain. Allow your heat to melt to be soft and moldable.

"Ezekiel 36:26 says, 'I will give you a new heart and a new spirit I will put within you. I will remove the heart of stone from your flesh and give you a heart of flesh.'

"Inhale for eight. Exhale for eight.

"Allow your heart of stone to crumble into a thousand tiny pieces like sand and then begin to feel God collect each speck. Every incident, picking it back up, and molding your heart back to a place of wholeness.

"Inhale for nine. Exhale for nine.

"Allow your belly to sink. Place your hand on your womb. In the literal sense, this is what sets us apart from men; the ability to conceive, to carry, and to deliver life in the natural; and in the spirit. We do the same in the spiritual realm. We are incubators holding our own dreams but also being the nudge to someone else's. When we birth God's purpose, we are equipped to reach back and help others do the same.

"Inhale for ten and exhale for ten.

"Today, I want you to set your intention on one specific thing, person, dream, event, goal, or prayer that you hope to have peace with, a solution for, or a word for, by the end of this session. Remember that out of your belly will flow rivers of living water. I want you to feel the stirring of possibility. The possibility that the vision was from Him. The possibility that the wound can be fixed. The possibility that you can be healed. The possibility that you can be free from worry, doubt, confusion, degradation, depression, low self-esteem, distraction, and emptiness. The possibility that God actually is God.

"Continue to breathe at whatever number is good for you. Maybe you're a three. Maybe you're a ten. This is your moment. Let it be what you need it to be.

"As you pay attention to your breath, begin to thank God that you are able to wiggle your toes, point and flex your feet, rotate your ankles, lift one leg and then the other.

"Shhhh. Open your ears so that you can hear the farthest sound in the room. I want you to bring it closer to you and closer to you. This is what God wants: for His voice to be the loudest that you hear. For Him to be so close that it sounds like a whisper in your ear. Whenever you're speaking to Him, He's communicating back with you. That you would not put more trust in the lies of the enemy that scream in your ears. But that you would hold the truth of God's Word to a higher level. The truth that He whispers to you.

"Hear His voice. It's quiet but it's stern. It's quiet but it's truth. It's quiet but it's love. It's the relationship that flows. It renews and restores. Like a child who can hear her daddy from a mile away, become like a child once again where He will restore you, and renew you where you would know without a shadow of a doubt that He is Lord, that He is God. If you trust just a tiny bit that He is able, whisper, 'I trust You.'

"Return back to your breath three, four, five . . .

"As you walk outside, you will notice the clouds, the sun, water, and changing trees. You don't have to physically touch the air or the clouds, or the water to know that it's real. To know that death is beyond our reach and to know that life lives in it. To know that it holds power, but it's balanced. Nothing you could do could change it. To know that it lives until God says otherwise. When the currents get high, still God. And day and night, still God. You are not affected unless you get into the water. Unless you feel the breeze on your skin, and unless you cross the threshold of sand and enter the fresh renewing water. We have to get in the water.

"As babies, the water of fluid in our mother's womb kept us comforted and safe in a place where we could hide and grow. Our organs could form. Our limbs could grow.

"God wants to rebirth you today. Build a covering now. Restoration of your mind, body, and spirit; and even your faith. If you can put your faith in the ocean, you can put your faith in the God that created it and controls it. He controls the wind and the waves.

"Matthew 8:27 says, and the men marveled saying, 'What sort of man is this that even winds and seas obey Him?'

"Sit at the edge of possibility. The endless ocean is the length of your possibility in God. Allow it to brush up on your feet; tickle the soles of your feet; grace your ankles and legs and come up even higher. Sometimes we only need a little bit more than fifty-one percent in order to go all the way. More than half-way. That is mustard seed faith. It's here that we begin to doubt though, but don't worry. You won't drown. You won't die. You won't fail. You're already there. You might as well go all the way.

"Return to a place of comfort. The place of the original planning. The original Word that was spoken to you. The original command that you were given. The original vision. Not a toe in but your whole self in. You have nothing to lose but the things that are keeping you in bondage. That's all that you have to lose. You have nothing to lose but the wounds that are already lifted from you.

"Trust: you have nothing to lose but barrenness that wasn't yours to begin with.

"Trust: you have nothing to lose but the lies that the enemy has used to keep you from accessing the truth of your relationship with God.

"Trust: you have nothing to lose but the patterns that keep you out of freely flowing with the will of God.

"I trust God because God is God.

"Your life is not yours. It's loaned to you. Walk in the water. Your feet, your knees, your hips, and now your womb. Float in His love. Allow it to fill the wounds.

Allow His grace to mend the empty places. Allow His mercy to cover the hurts and pain that prevented you from going all the way with Him before.

"As you are now full, fall all the way into the ocean. The sea of His love. Keep falling and falling until every ounce is filled with Him. Allow the weight of His glory to make the great exchange, turning your mourning into dancing. Allow yourself to feel weightless. Sinking but not in a bad way; but in a sense of baptism when you are trusting that God is God. God is everything that you need Him to be in this moment. Call Him what you need to call Him. If you need a father, call Him. If you need a mother, call Him. If you need peace, call Him. He is the great El Shaddai, the Lord Almighty. He is Yahweh, Lord Jehovah. He is Jehovah Nisi, your banner. He is Jehovah Raffa, the Lord that heals. He is Jehovah Shammah, the Lord is here. Elohim, the everlasting God. Jehovah Jireh, the God who provides. Jehovah Sholom, the Lord is peace. Jehovah Saba, the Lord of Hosts.

"Call out what you need Him to be. Feel the renewness of your heart. You have the heart of Christ that flows fruits of His Spirit. Feel the renewing of your mind as you sink deeper and deeper into the realization of who God is.

"God is God. God is everything. There is nothing you

cannot do without Him. You can do all things through Christ that strengthens you. Allow His strength to be your joy. Feel the rejuvenation of your body. You were made in His image, which is whole.

"God is God.

"Inhale. Exhale. Open your eyes as you ascend back to the top of the water. And as you walk back onto the sand, you are made new.

"Place your hand on your womb. The stirring is now happening. The things that you have dreamed of are coming to reality. God's light is shining on you in this moment. Everything that you need is at your fingertips. All you have to do is say it and believe it, and it is yours.

"God is God. I trust God."

By the conclusion of the retreat, God had spoken so clearly and succinctly to my spirit, every inkling of doubt was removed. Every facet of fear was abolished. Every mountain of shame and insecurity was brought low.

All the while, I asked God to empty my wounded yet yielded vessel. To realign it and refill it with the power of His glorious Holy Spirit. I needed my husband to know and trust that I would honor, respect, and submit to him as God's Word has instructed, and as I have vowed to do.

When I left home for the retreat, our family was contending with a serious criminal matter. When I returned, I was once again standing in the middle of a tug-of-war between my husband and my son. The outcome would prove irreparable to their relationship, and near devastation between my husband and I. Though our marriage would survive, there'd be a gaping hole in my heart.

With a tremendous amount of peace, I texted the following to my husband:

> "There is just one thing I'd like you to consider. Pray about it and think about it while you're at church. For all that I've experienced this weekend, for all that I've surrendered and given to God, for myself, our marriage, and our family to be realigned, for the fruitfulness of our blended family, for our marriage's ministry mission, would you consider talking to Justin and dropping all charges? All I can do is ask. You don't even have to answer me. In fact, don't. Just prepare your heart. Commune with your Lord. And, act as you will. I'd rather not know your decision. I'll wait and watch God work because

I surrendered this weekend, and I totally and fully trust God. I've realigned myself to God first, you second, and our children third. That's what I'm instructed to do as a Christian, wife, and mother. I can only be responsible for me, my thoughts, and my actions, and no one else. God sees my heart, your heart, Justin's heart, and Joshua's heart. When I left Friday, they were all wounded and broken. I know at least one that's been mended. I love you with every fiber of my being. I pray and continue to pray, and have fasted, and will continue to fast, and I asked God specifically to show me how to manifest my heart's desire to you. While preparing to get in the shower, this is what He instructed me to do and say. I am His obedient servant. With all my love . . ."

On an exceptionally warm and sunny Sunday, September afternoon, I communed with my Lord on a sixty-minute car ride home. I praised, worshipped, prayed, and listened to His voice. After a warm reception by Kelvin and Joshua, I came to this realization:

Revelation

There comes a time when you need to get away from life's daily distractions:

To spend quality time with God;

To commune with like-minded and goal-oriented women to pursue the heart of God;

To contend in the spirit, and come into agreement with what God's Word says and promises to be true;

To reset your mind, body, and spirit in complete alignment with Him;

To empty your vessel in great expectation of refilling to overflowing;

To have your head, hands, and feet anointed with oil;

To give your all to Him in total and complete surrender;

To submit to His perfect and intentional will for your life;

To purify your heart in preparation for the Encounter;

To present yourself as a living, sacrificial bride to Him, your bBridegroom;

And to partake of His body and drink of His blood in remembrance of His ultimate sacrifice of love toward you.

God has given each of us life that we might fulfill His individually assigned purpose, will, and intent. There is a problem you were created to solve. One to which only you have been given the answer.

Over the past ten years, I have discovered that my role as a mother was not to control to the point of conformity, but to influence to the point of self-sufficiency. My role is to be a voice of primary, positive influence. That voice is present from birth until death. Its functional application may change, but its audibility does not.

In the formative years, that voice is understood as the role of caretaker. One who is responsible for maintenance, supervision, and custody. For reassuring object permanence, easing stranger anxiety, and allowing prowess through the typical twos. Or setting boundaries, establishing order, and expressing morals. It is through this voice that a child learns love, trust, and security.

Through preadolescence, our voices are stern and intentional. They may liken us to cops; the great Sherlock Holmes. We *see* things that are, according to them, not meant to be seen: the unmade bed; clothes on the floor; and the five minutes past the TV, social media, or cell phone limit. While, according to them, we *do not see* that they are the only ones not allowed to loiter aimlessly at the local mall, have a boyfriend/girlfriend, or purchase the hottest pair of one-hundred-fifty-dollar sneakers. Like we just don't understand them. To them, we are so lame. We're so busy making sure we point out every household rule they've broken, and hand out tickets complete with appropriate consequences, that we fail to see and treasure the heart of what they're struggling with at this age. While policing our children, our voices must proactively teach the importance of civil responsibility, public safety, and the relationship between actions and consequences.

Through high school and late adolescence, our voices should develop into ones that train, instruct, and advise in the manner of a coach. Your child should desire your guidance in the same way an athlete desires their coach's. Your advice should be positive, knowledgeable, and goal-oriented, and it should be perceived as supportive, respectful, and distinctively clear. Children need and crave instruction. When spoken gently, your voice teaches them discipline and self-control in preparation to win.

Once your child has mastered winning, your voice of influence serves as consultant. You've been parenting long enough to give professional and expert advice. In whatever situation your children find themselves, your expertise will serve them well. You may not have traveled the same road nor experienced the same insult, but you can use the tragedy of your past to help them live a triumphant future. It does not mean they will live an innocuous life. But using wisdom, it could be one less burden. It is through this voice that your adult child learns to improve their performance in terms of personal leadership, stewardship, and profitability.

The final area in which your voice serves as a primary influence is as confidante. At this point, your child is an early adult or middle-aged, and quite likely a parent in their own right. In literature, a confidante is a secondary character, often an authority figure or friend, whose role is to listen to the secrets of the protagonist, examine their character, and advise them on their actions. Is that not what the adult parent-child relationship illustrates? Your voice is empathetic, trustworthy, and nonjudgmental. In this terminal role, you will have taught perspective, accountability, and integrity.

In all of this, I would hope that my life has both reflected and taught integrity: a collection of virtues inclusive of honesty, courage, honor, respect, responsibility, restraint, and authenticity.

Testimony

Travail: to toil and exert oneself in painfully difficult and burdensome work; to endure through anguish and suffering; to labor; to deliver; to birth.

From the time the sun rises on one season, and sets on the same, there exists space sufficient for work to be done.

There was a darkly, enlightening season through which I travailed. Had it not been for a group of God-ordained midwives, my seed would have been aborted.

Through their guided support, I travailed through the first stages of labor, and am now positioned to push, and deliver God's intentionally purposed vision.

God positioned me strategically. The bag of intravenous fluids is in, the epidural has taken, I am completely dilated and fully effaced; my feet are in the stirrups; it's time to *push*!

For me, nothing comes to commencement nor completion without first hearing His voice. He has spoken loudly and clearly.

I am realigned and ready to level up.

We are Blended Beyond Expectation!

DEVOTIONAL ANECDOTE:

A LESSON FROM A SINFUL WOMAN

†

The story of this sinful woman is one centered on unselfish love and sacrifice.

Luke 7:36–50 (NIV)

When one of the Pharisees invited Jesus to have dinner with him, he went to the Pharisee's house and reclined at the table. A woman in that town, who lived a sinful life, learned that Jesus was eating at the Pharisee's house, so she came there with an alabaster jar of perfume. As she stood behind him at his feet weeping, she began to wet his feet with her tears. Then she wiped them with her hair, kissed them, and poured perfume on them.

When the Pharisees who had invited him saw this, he said to himself, "If this man were a prophet, he would know who is touching him and what kind of woman she is—that she is a sinner."

Jesus answered him, "Simon, I have something to tell you."

"Tell me, teacher," he said.

"Two people owed money to a certain moneylender. One owed him five hundred denarii, and the other fifty. Neither of them had the money to pay him back, so he forgave the debts of both. Now which of them will love him more?"

Simon replied, "I suppose the one who had the bigger debt forgiven."

"You have judged correctly," Jesus said.

Then he turned toward the woman and said to Simon, "Do you see this woman? I came into your house. You did not give me any water for my feet, but she wet my feet with her tears and wiped them with her hair. You did not give me a kiss, but this woman, from the time I entered, has not stopped kissing my feet. Therefore, I tell you, her many sins have been forgiven as her great love has shown. But whoever has been forgiven little loves little."

Then Jesus said to her, "Your sins are forgiven."

The other guests began to say among themselves: "Who is this who even forgives sins?"

Jesus said to the woman, "Your faith has saved you; go in peace."

Simon hosted a feast to which this woman was not invited. She was an unclean sinner who would have been prohibited from serving in the local synagogue. Her sin was not identified nor was it supposed. She was shunned, looked down upon, humiliated, and disrespected. Her opinion was neither sought after nor regarded. She was inwardly wounded and outwardly ashamed.

She heard Jesus was coming, and like the woman with the issue of blood, who needed only to touch the hem of His garment, she simply wanted to be in His presence. She too desired wholeness and restoration.

How did she get in? How was it that this discarded woman was invisible to the Pharisaical elite? Why didn't Simon exclude her from his home?

She was waiting inside when Jesus arrived.

Though not necessarily required, providing a basin to wash the dust off one's feet, offering scented oil to anoint a guest's hair, and greeting beloved guests with a kiss would have been warmly received. Simon offered none of these as a gracious host.

But this sinful woman washed Jesus's feet with her

tears, dried them with her hair, kissed them, and finally anointed them with expensive perfume. All as an act of deep reverence. Her love was displayed by acts of honor.

Simon's appall was *not* that Jesus was being touched, but by *whom*. Thankfully, Jesus was not a respecter of persons. He did not show favoritism. He would dine with the religious elite alongside the sinner.

Using a parable of debtors as an example, Jesus asked Simon, who would love the moneylender more? His right reply was: the one who's greatest debt had been forgiven. Jesus lovingly told the woman her sins were forgiven.

Any one of us could be this sinful woman. She is a nameless example of self-worth through forgiveness and not of righteous living. Sometimes we are not looking for forgiveness from others but from ourselves. I was that sinful woman.

I was emotionally broken and spiritually wounded, searching for healing and restoration through an intimate act of reverence. I washed His feet with my tears, dried them with my hair, kissed them, and anointed them with the priceless perfume of surrender, adoration, and awe.

I came to Him out of gratitude and acceptance of His unconditional love and forgiveness. I am eternally grateful for the One who let me in and allowed me to stay.

QUESTIONS TO CONSIDER

1. Are you satisfied with your alignment?
2. From what voice of influence do you normally speak?
3. What does your voice of influence say about you?
4. What will be your legacy of influence?

WORDS OF ENCOURAGEMENT

There is no success without failure.

SONG FOR YOUR SEASON

"Alabaster Box"—CeCe Winans

ACT OF KINDNESS

Allow yourself to breathe and let God handle it.

EPILOGUE
†

As I travel this road called life, I've come to appreciate the views along this journey. In some places the landscape is created by the long broad stokes of perseverance through tribulation, while others showcase the delicate touch of faith through acceptance. No matter the brush, the outcome is a beautifully composed painting that tells the story of the Artist who's in control of every stroke.

Unlike a novel, a memoir does not end. It continues to evolve, and family is no different. The main body of my story ended in 2011, with the final chapter culminating in a personal epiphany in September 2019. During the interim between 2011 and now, this happened:

Steffon graduated from a trade school in the Greater Philadelphia area with a concentration in carpentry. He is working to build his own business as an independent contractor. Now twenty-six, he is married to his high school sweetheart, Chelsi. They have two precious children: Zuri and Asar. Steffon's relationship with his father is healthy and growing.

Justin's journey was different. After high school he attended a local community college before transferring to a university in Central Florida, where he studied recording arts and sound engineering. Moving to Florida and living on his own afforded him a new start. He decided to go by the name Eli; Elijah is his middle name. He realized college wasn't for him. He never liked school, and therefore dropped out. He completed a certification program in Pro Tools, a music software, at a recording studio in Atlanta, Georgia, and is a certified audio engineer.

Eli works odd jobs here and there while engineering sound for his own music as an up-and-coming recording artist. He is twenty-five and in a loving relationship with his girlfriend, Ashley. She has a daughter, Luna, and, in 2020, they welcomed their daughter Nola. His relationship with Kelvin is optimistic.

Joshua is a one-of-a-kind gem of a thirteen-year-old who is amusingly clever and full of wit beyond his years. He is an honor student and loves everything pertaining to basketball and the Seattle Seahawks. He still allows public displays of affection and is delighted to see me home every Thursday after school. He often wonders why his brothers are so much older than him and why he has never experienced being fussed with when, at bedtime, he is found giggling with his siblings instead of sleeping. In due time he will understand the blessing of our blending!

Kelvin and I continue to mature and grow through the lessons that marriage teaches.

Our blending has afforded us the opportunity to share, encourage, and inspire in ways we could not have done otherwise.

NOTES
†

CHAPTER TWO: INAUGURATION DAY

"Whenever God wants to bring . . . enough to handle the answer."

Grady, J. Lee. 2012. *Fearless Daughters of the Bible.* Bloomington: Chosen Books.

CHAPTER FOUR: STOP RUNNING THROUGH THE WOODS

"Worship is where we find . . . when we look to Him."

Grady, J. Lee. 2012. *Fearless Daughters of the Bible.* Bloomington: Chosen Books.

CHAPTER SIX: LETTERS FROM THE HEART

"Boldness is a great virtue . . . and that He will answer."

Grady, J. Lee. 2012. *Fearless Daughters of the Bible.* Bloomington: Chosen Books.

CHAPTER SEVEN: UNCOMMON FAVOR

"(I) was willing to surrender . . . me according to Your word."

Grady, J. Lee. 2012. *Fearless Daughters of the Bible.* Bloomington: Chosen Books.

Connect with me on social media:
LinkedIn: Naomi L Hill Hugh MD
Facebook: Naomi L Hill Hugh MD
Instagram: naomilhillhughmd
Email: DrNaomiLHillHugh@gmail.com

CPSIA information can be obtained
at www.ICGtesting.com
Printed in the USA
BVHW040159191020
591312BV00018B/557